Few parents are as fortunate
as I have been to be the father of
Corrie, Bob, Holly, Ryan,
Kelly, and Emmalee.
Thanks to each of them for
letting me reach for the stars.

FIRST CHANCE

**How Kids
With Nothing
Can Change
Everything**

Robert Owen Carr
with Dirk Johnson

TABLE OF CONTENTS

ACKNOWLEDGMENTS

The powerful stories in this book could not have been told without the courage of the young people who shared their painful memories and difficult circumstances. They richly deserve their triumphs.

Their families, too, exhibited remarkable generosity of heart in opening their homes and talking honestly about their lives, even in cases that involved shame and remorse. They deserve solace and pride in the cause of compassion, hope, and opportunity.

The students and their families merit appreciation, too, for their many examples of love, loyalty, determination, and in some cases, their inspiring search for recovery and redemption.

Though their names do not appear in the book, many current and former Give Back students were helpful with their insights about overcoming hardship. These include Tatiana Mickens, Elijah Kelsey, Larry Mensah, Kimberly Gould, Frances Brodeur, and Marquis Vega.

Other foster children have aged out of the system many decades ago, but were indelibly shaped by their experience, like Robert Price, now in his fifties, a foster kid who found his way. He contributed insights that mightily helped our efforts.

I am deeply grateful to Kathie Hanratty, who helped shape the focus of the book. Her support has been enormously meaningful.

This book draws on the wisdom of those who have dedicated their careers to foster children, the homeless, and the incarcerated and their children. A handful of these heroes in the field include Peter Samuelson, Sara Goldrick-Rab, Angela Duckworth, Rebecca Ginsburg, Doris Houston, and Paige Chan. In addition, the book gained from the insights of experts at Chapin Hall at the University of Chicago, the National Children of Incarcerated Parents Conference – Arizona State University, and Born This Way Foundation – Lady Gaga and Cynthia Germanotta.

A very large contribution from Peter and Veronica Mallouk made it possible for Give Back to establish a program in our seventh and latest state, Kansas. Their kindness and generosity leave me humbled.

I am appreciative for the help of prison officials who allowed access to their facilities. I am especially grateful to the authorities at the Cumberland County Jail in New Jersey, who allowed me to step inside and talk to inmates about their lives and struggles. I am deeply appreciative for the cooperation of authorities at the Arizona State Prison Complex-Perryville. I am thankful, as well, to the authorities at the Edna Mahan Correctional Facility in Union Township, New Jersey. Thanks, too, for the insights and candor of Carolyn Gurski, as chief of women's division for the Illinois Department of Corrections, who accommodated our access to the Decatur Correctional Center and the Logan Correctional Center. I also extend my sincere appreciation to the incarcerated persons who spoke with me.

It is impossible to name every Give Back mentor around the country who has stood at the shoulder of these students, but the remarkable contributions of John Fuqua must surely be noted.

I thank the foster parents who care for these young people, as well as the devoted volunteers of CASA who look out for children in need.

The Give Back program would not be possible without the commitment of our college partners:

California State University, San Bernardino, Chapman University, and University of La Verne in California;

University of Delaware;

Blackburn College, Illinois State University, Lewis University, Northern Illinois University, University of Illinois, and the University of St. Francis in Illinois;

Baker University, Kansas State University, Pittsburg State University, and Wichita State University in Kansas;

Montclair State University, New Jersey Institute of Technology, Rowan University, Rowan College at Gloucester County, St. Peter's University, The College of New Jersey, and William Paterson University in New Jersey;

Binghamton University, Mercy College, and Queens College in New York;

Elizabethtown College, Kutztown University, University of the Sciences, West Chester University, and Williamson College of the Trades in Pennsylvania.

For this book and for so many other important matters, I rely strongly on the support and wisdom of our Give Back board members: Susan Herbst-Murphy, John Murphy, Jonathan Watson, Michael Parker, and Richard Clemens.

I am grateful to the University of Illinois Press, especially Michael Roux, for its prestigious imprimatur as the distributor of this book.

Our staff members at Give Back, in so many ways, have championed our young scholars. These esteemed colleagues include Melissa Helmbrecht, Dr. Amy Young, Steve Cardamone, Robert Tucker, Kevin O'Donnell, Joshua Meekins, Domenic Merendino, Darrell Edmonds, Lina Moe, Lydia Matlock, Jonathan Pugh, Christine Brown, Jessica Finkbiner, Julie Branchaw, Jessica Nichols, Katie Latta, Christian Oberly, Mark Melka, Erika Tucker, and Amber Young. Ivy Cohen, of Beyond, was also invaluable.

I stand awestruck by their talents. I am deeply grateful for our shared sense of mission.

For our Give Back alumni scholars, I am forever grateful and proud. Their astonishing rates of college graduation prove that our program works.

PREFACE

They might be called America's forgotten kids. They are everywhere, and yet, they are largely invisible to most of us. These young people rarely talk about family circumstances that are viewed as wrong or shameful, even though they are blameless themselves.

Some 2.7 million children in America have a parent in jail or prison. About 1.6 million kids have endured homelessness. On any given day, some 437,000 kids are in foster care, a figure that grew significantly in the era of the opioid crisis.

If we count the *uncounted*—the children of absent or struggling parents who live informally with relatives or friends—the number of displaced kids is much higher.

At a time when higher education of some kind has become a virtual prerequisite for financial stability, the graduation rate for kids from troubled backgrounds is scandalously low.

Only an estimated 50 percent of foster youth graduate from high school and less than 10 percent obtain a bachelor's degree, according to an analysis by the *Hechinger Report*.

Among students of economic and social hardship who do manage to gain admission to college, the cost of housing, food, transportation, and fees can be overwhelming, even in cases when tuition is minimal or waived entirely.

LGBT kids are disproportionately represented among foster and homeless youth, often because they have been rejected by biological or foster parents for their sexual orientation or gender identity. These young homeless people are especially vulnerable to predators and the "survivor sex" that is sometimes traded in exchange for shelter.

Decades of rising rates of female incarceration, meanwhile, has severely destabilized many families. While women account for only 8 percent of prison inmates, female incarceration has grown dramatically in recent decades, even as male incarceration has begun to decline. By some estimates, some 80 percent of incarcerated women are mothers. Since 1978, the jailing of women has grown eightfold.

The trauma and upheaval tend to be especially devastating for children when a mother goes to jail. When a father is incarcerated, children stay with mothers in about 90 percent of cases, according to a study by the Annie E. Casey Foundation. But when a mother is imprisoned, kids in about 50 percent of the cases are shuffled among the homes of relatives – often a grandmother – or placed in the state welfare system.

When women return from prison, moreover, they tend to face condemnation more severe than men experience, according to prison officials and psychologists. For the children, it can mean losing a relationship with their mothers, and being sent to foster home after foster home.

When foster kids age out of the system and state payments cease for guardians—at age eighteen or twenty-one, depending on the state—many of these children struggle to survive on their own.

Among children of incarcerated parents, financial and emotional difficulties often start early. When a mom or dad is handcuffed and led away by police, it is commonplace for kids to have been watching. Many of these children, meanwhile, fall into a trap of thinking they are destined to follow the same path.

"When I acted up, people told me I was going to turn out just like my mom—on drugs and in jail," said Sarah, a high school freshman whose mother was locked up. "And you know something? I worried that they were right."

These kids face harsh economic realities. The Russell Sage Foundation found that the incarceration of a family member was associated with a 64 percent decline in household assets, a devastating blow to those who were already struggling.

It is little wonder that so many of them experience mental and physical health problems, and run-ins with the law. Still others are expected to financially help support a parent or a sibling, even if they do not live together, a burden that makes college attendance almost impossible.

What *is* remarkable is that so many of these young people defy the expectations and attain success. All of them, whether they achieve financial and educational heights or not, teach powerful lessons about survival and will, courage and grace.

Imagine how many more could soar—if only they were given a first chance.

I grew up in a troubled household. My father was a hard-drinking, bitter man who belittled and knocked me around. He served at least a couple of stints behind bars, although I was not living in the house at the time. My mother worked the night shift as a waitress to help feed her six children.

Neither of my parents wanted me to go to college. When I unexpectedly received a $250 college scholarship during my senior year at Lockport Township High School in Illinois, in 1963, I was inspired that someone believed in me and thought I was worth an investment. I vowed then that I would do the same for other kids, if I ever had extra money.

It took many years of struggle, but I finally achieved success in a big way. In 2003, I founded an organization that came to be known as Give Something Back. I have invested in more than 1,500 college scholarships and have provided mentoring services for students who have known hardship. The organization has grown from a single high school, my alma mater, and now reaches students in seven states.

I was chagrined to learn about the extremely low rate of college graduation among students who had experienced foster care, homelessness, or the incarceration of a parent, especially the mother.

I shifted the focus of the program to make a special outreach to these students—kids with so many hurdles—and so much talent.

ROC

CHAPTER ONE

PINKY PROMISES

To the baristas in the Starbucks at the Cumberland Mall, Mercedes Marquez was a regular, the polite and cheerful high school kid who spent hours just hanging out, sipping a Very Berry Hibiscus, and working away on her laptop.

Mercedes seemed the picture of innocence, a carefree American teen.

Her classmates had elected her president of the freshman class. She had been a soccer star before being sidelined by an injury. Now a junior, she studied hard, made good grades, and steered clear of alcohol and drugs. She hoped to go off to college and make a life somewhere beyond her small hometown of Millville, New Jersey. She dreamed of becoming a journalist.

"I want to be on the scene," she said with a grin. "I want to be the person who explains what's going on in the world."

Mercedes had been searching for some good explanations for as long as she could remember. Although the baristas might never have guessed it, this was a girl who had struggled to elbow her way through dire circumstances most of her life.

Just maybe, Mercedes mused, things were about to take a turn for the better. Christmas was drawing near. She had made some trusted friends. And her mom had just been released from jail.

Mercedes did not remember a time in her life without cops, jail, and chaos. At the age of five, she was zooming in a stolen car with her mother in a wild high-speed police chase. It ended when the vehicle crashed into a tree. Mercedes was physically unharmed, but was left scared and confused as she watched her mother being taken away by the police. Her father, for his part, had been mostly out of the picture, save for a random call every once in the bluest of moons.

Her mom, Angie, was a heroin addict. For most of Mercedes's life, she had been in and out of county jail and state prison, including three stints at the notorious Edna Mahan women's correctional facility in New Jersey.

Angie, in her early thirties, looked so drawn and frighteningly thin that people wondered how she was able to walk.

She had lost her way a long time ago.

As Angie put it: "People say, 'I would never put a needle in my arm.' 'I would never steal.' 'I would never stand on the corner and sell myself.'"

All my nevers came true.

She fell silent and stared at the floor.

"You can call me a bad mom," said Angie, a plastic crucifix hanging from her neck. "I blame myself. People get so upset about losing their house or car. But your pride, your dignity, that's what's hard to lose."

Like so many people who end up addicted and imprisoned, Angie had lived through a hellish childhood herself.

"The man I grew up calling 'Dad' poured gasoline on the floor and threatened to light a match," she said. "He beat my mother so bad she was hospitalized. He pulled a gun on her. He chased me with a baseball bat."

Her stepfather ultimately went to prison for murder. Angie's troubled mom, meanwhile, was left to support the children on her own. Her mother often worked eighteen hours a day, a grind that meant leaving the kids on their own much of the time.

"She did the best she could."

Angie was fifteen when she got pregnant with Mercedes and dropped out of school. Her boyfriend was twenty. She started using the hallucinogenic drug ecstasy when Mercedes was a baby. By the time Angie was seventeen, she was shooting heroin and selling drugs.

Almost from the beginning, she saw the look of disappointment in the eyes of her daughter. When Mercedes was a little girl, Angie would make "pinky promises" with her. "I'm not going to get high anymore," or "I promise I'm going to come back tonight."

She broke her word almost every time. She had been through rehab perhaps a dozen times, sometimes getting high again as soon as she walked out of a treatment facility. She had overdosed more than once. She had even flatlined.

As a little girl, Mercedes saw too much.

"Mom was always mad," she said, "because I'd say something at school that she wanted to keep secret."

There was the time, for example, that Mercedes found a syringe and asked her first-grade teacher about it.

"Why does my mommy do that?" Mercedes asked her grandmother. "She doesn't love me. She doesn't want to be my mommy."

It wasn't long before Mercedes stopped talking about her mother. When her mother's name came up, Mercedes would leave the room.

Letters to Mercedes from her mother in jail would mostly go unopened. The girl declared that she was done with her mom, once and for all. The woman had chosen drugs over her family. It seemed that nothing was ever going to change.

But even as she grew older, and the troubles worsened, Mercedes never really stopped caring about her mother. She wanted to believe her.

"My mom *tells* me she loves me," said Mercedes.

During a discussion in a classroom at school one day, there was talk about a powerful and dangerous new substance on the street. Mercedes promptly went to her grandmother with a worried look.

"When you talk to my mom, please tell her to be careful of this new kind of heroin," she told her. "It's called 'pink.'"

It was a role reversal common in families with a parent disabled by drugs or depression. The child takes on grown-up responsibilities and tries desperately to guide a mom or dad in the right direction.

"Mercedes tries to be my mom," said Angie, who had been scolded by her daughter for dressing provocatively. "She asks me what I'm wearing before I go out. She'll say, 'Don't wear your tights!'"

Mercedes also looked out for her little brother, Marcus, who lived with an aunt. For Christmas, she bought him a pair of basketball shoes that the boy had been coveting. But she knew he needed more than just the shoes. He needed the love and approval of his mother.

Mercedes had an idea. She told her mother she would "go halves" with her on the cost of the shoes, but wanted the present to come from the mom alone. When Marcus opened the gift and the card from his mom, he was delighted and surprised. Mercedes, faithful to her mission, reacted with surprise, too, silent that she had anything to do with the gift.

Since she was little, Mercedes had lived with her grandmother, Debbie Futrell. She called her "Mom Maw," a combination of mom and grandma, which seemed to be an apt name for her combined role.

For most of her working life, her grandmother had cleaned rooms at casinos in Atlantic City–often doing double shifts–before being diagnosed with emphysema. She also suffered with severe mental health problems, including bipolar depression.

Even as an older woman, Debbie engaged in self-harm by cutting herself. She attributed the act of painful self-mutilation to her guilt over the troubled life and early death of another daughter, Michelle, a drug addict. When Michelle did not come home at night, her mother would venture out into the darkness to search for her, sometimes forcing her way into the crack houses of Millville.

She could not save her. The young woman died after being run over by a car. In a brief article about the death, the local newspaper referred to her daughter as merely "a known prostitute."

The depression and mood swings of Mom Maw made every day unpredictable for Mercedes. The girl would look for clues as soon as her grandmother picked her up after school.

"If she says 'Hi' when I get in the car, I know things will probably go okay," she said. "But if she doesn't say anything, and just sits there quietly, staring straight ahead, I know it's not going to be good."

After school and on weekends, Mercedes worked at two jobs, Taco Bell and Aeropostale. Depending on the size of her paycheck, she gave her grandmother a big share of the money to help pay the bills.

They lived near Main Street, where a sign proclaimed Millville as *The Holly City of America*. But the town looked more despairing than merry. Many of the houses were boarded and empty. Vacant lots were strewn with shards of glass and choked with weeds.

Her grandmother's apartment was on the second floor of a building that was badly in need of paint and repairs. The stairway was unlit and several spindles were missing from the banister. A sheet was draped over one of the windows.

There was a church in the neighborhood, and Mercedes would go alone to services on Sundays. She liked a Bible passage that said all of God's children were beloved.

Her old first-grade teacher had taken her to the church's summer camp when Mercedes was younger. At the camp, she learned some comforting words: *No matter what you go through, or who you lose, you've always got God.*

"I don't know if that's true," Mercedes said, "but through my darkest times, I've gotten through with hope."

Mercedes was spending a lot of time thinking—and hoping—about college. She was stumped, though, about how she would ever find the money for tuition and room and board. She believed that she could compete successfully in the classroom. And she felt certain that college could transform her life. She believed that getting an education could end this awful family ritual of drugs and jail and poverty.

Some of her streetwise cousins winced at Mercedes's straitlaced behavior, her bookish interests, and her ambitious notions about college. They suspected that she thought of herself as superior.

When they gave Mercedes guff, their grandmother would step in and explain to the cousins that she did not regard herself as better than them, just different. She had simply chosen another path.

Mercedes had been steadfast in showing her love and loyalty to the family. When one of the teenage cousins, Zeb, overdosed on heroin, and lay in a hospital bed on life support for a month before he died, it was Mercedes who stood at his side, held his hand, and washed and combed his hair.

Too many members of her family had followed a path to jail or the graveyard.

Her grandmother had been encouraging Mercedes to consider the military, where money wouldn't be a concern. It came with risks, sure, but so did living in a dicey neighborhood of Millville. And life in the military offered a lot of benefits and security.

Mercedes went with her grandmother to visit a military recruiting office in town. A broad-shouldered soldier in a crisp blue uniform with brass buttons—he looked to Mercedes like the hunky wrestler-turned-actor John Cena—delivered a powerful pitch. The recruiter told her she could realize all of her dreams in the military. He said she could become a journalist for military periodicals. And he told her she would be able to start her career right away. She wouldn't need to bother getting a bachelor's degree.

The minimum age to join the military was eighteen, he said, but with the consent of a legal guardian, she could start at seventeen. That was coming up in the summer.

"I think the military would be good for you," her grandmother told her when they were back at the apartment.

Mercedes told her she appreciated all of the selling points of the armed forces.

"But I think college would be pretty cool, too," she said, sitting cross-legged on the living room couch in a Penn State sweatshirt. "No one in our family has ever gone away to college."

Angie's sobriety since her release from jail, meanwhile, had stretched through Christmas. Mercedes was feeling as good about her mother – and life in general – as she had in a long time. Her mom was living with a sister, but she and Mercedes were now talking regularly and texting several times a day.

Her mom swore she was going to stay clean. She was determined to show she could be the mom Mercedes had needed and deserved for so long.

"I can't just *ask* her to respect me anymore," Angie acknowledged. "I have to *earn* it."

Angie had landed a job, cleaning offices in town. She surprised her daughter by telling her she would like to help her shop for a dress for prom in the spring. Mercedes thanked her mom and told her how much that would mean to her.

"Mercedes is being wonderful," her grandmother observed. "She's trying to give her mother a chance. This is as close as they've ever been."

In the living room of her grandmother's apartment, an old photograph hanging on the wall showed Angie with her arms wrapped around Mercedes and Marcus. Nearby a sign was printed with the words: *Think good thoughts.*

Mercedes could not help but daydream about
happy possibilities:

> *My mom will stay clean and we'll get a place of our own.*
> *She won't need to be with guys. The family will be enough.*
> *She'll come to my school events. I won't have to explain*
> *to people why I live with my grandma. I won't get anxiety*
> *and embarrassment every Mother's Day when people ask*
> *me what we did to celebrate.*

It had been fifty-six days of sobriety for her mom —
nearly two months without any crack or heroin.

She relapsed on New Year's Day.

CHAPTER TWO

ZIP CODE RULES

New Jersey, where I live, ranks as one of the wealthier places in America. Million-dollar houses are plentiful in northern parts of the state, home to executives who work at the headquarters of Fortune 500 companies, such as Johnson & Johnson, Merck, Prudential, and Honeywell. Many other residents in the region commute across the Hudson River to high-paying jobs in law offices and corporate suites in Manhattan.

Growing up with affluence might not count for everything. But it counts for quite a bit. In much of northern New Jersey, like the prosperous suburban counties of Hunterdon, Morris, Somerset, and Bergen, parents with money, like me, can help children burnish resumes with violin lessons and hire tutors to help achieve lofty scores on college admission exams.

South Jersey is another story.

In Cumberland County, ramshackle and weather-worn old homes have been carved into small apartments. Sheets of plywood cover the windows of some houses. These barricaded places sit empty, except when used as a "shooting gallery" for heroin addicts or as a hideaway for drug dealers. The homes have fallen into foreclosure and nobody much wants to buy them.

Jim Watson, senior vice president of the Cumberland County Improvement Authority, put it this way:

"About half of the county's population lives in Bridgeton, Vineland, and Millville – three little cities with big city problems – and the other half of the county is mostly rural and poor."

With the highest poverty rate of any county in New Jersey, Cumberland had the highest rate of high school dropouts, the highest percentage of teenage pregnancies, and the highest rate of children placed in the child welfare system.

"We're first in all of the categories," Watson lamented, "that you don't want to be first in."

The region, once a major center of glass manufacturing, had lost many of its better-paying jobs to cheaper labor and automation. A leading industry in the region nowadays was incarceration. More than 30 percent of all New Jersey inmates were housed in one of the five correctional facilities in Cumberland, even though the county's population of 155,000 was less than 2 percent of people living in the state.

Commerce Street, a main thoroughfare in the county seat of Bridgeton, became home to shuttered storefronts, secondhand shops, and social service outreach centers for those in need.

One of these old buildings bore the engraved name *Ashley*. That was also the name of a five-year-old girl in a homeless shelter—who through her love and willingness to accept love long ago—helped save the life of a struggling high school kid named Melissa Helmbrecht.

Many years later, Melissa and her husband, Wally Kappeler, would move back to their native South Jersey from California to devote themselves to helping kids and their families. When they discovered the empty building inscribed with the name Ashley, it seemed like a beacon. They signed a lease and set to work in what might be called a child rescue operation.

Melissa had grown up in a troubled family. She endured anorexia and depression and spent time at a center for troubled adolescents. She failed the ninth and tenth grades.

For a high school project, Melissa volunteered at a homeless shelter and met little Ashley, and the two of them connected deeply.

"Until then, I had felt like a failure at everything I had done," said Melissa. "But this little girl taught me that I *did* have something to contribute."

In an astonishing turnaround, Melissa would become an honors student and a debate champion. While still in high school, she gave speeches at forums about her phoenix-like rise.

Melissa won acceptance to a private college, and after graduation, she was admitted to law school in Colorado. She would go on to a blazing career, with a stint at NASA and a promising business start-up in California. But something was missing.

She found the missing piece in the drafty old building named Ashley, with its creaky floorboards and scuffed walls. She and Wally made it a headquarters for helping endangered kids. Melissa led CASA (Court Appointed Special Advocates) and formed Stronger Families, a program to help those with incarcerated family members. Wally became the superintendent of a small school and director of the South Jersey chapter of the First Star Academy, which served foster children, and Melissa joined the cause.

In the First Star program, kids gathered on Saturdays in the Ashley building for recreation and skill-building sessions. It became a place for the foster children to bond with peers who knew the feeling of being shuffled from home to home.

Once a month, the group of thirty students would gather at Rowan University for academic grounding, inspirational talks, and socializing. In the summer, they took part in a six-week college immersion program at Rowan to hone academic skills. One summer they even took a trip to Florida, where they got a chance to visit Disney World, as well as do service work for a homeless shelter, the same place where young Melissa had met little Ashley so many years ago.

First Star became a safe haven for Cumberland County foster kids like Desiree and Anthony, Haley and Will.

Will Denson, with a warm smile and a voice that barely rose above a whisper, grew up thinking of jail as simply that place his mother was staying whenever she did not come home.

When he was eleven years old, Will and his brother were sent to live with an uncle, an ill-tempered man who viewed his nephews as burdens. He turned them into servants—and punching bags. When Will and his brother came home from school, they would be given a long list of chores that usually kept them toiling until bedtime.

"Scrubbing the floors, cleaning the toilet, you name it," Will recounted.

More than once, Will and his brother were awakened in the middle of the night by their uncle, high on drugs and fired with rage. In one of those terrifying times, at about two o'clock in the morning, the boys heard their uncle burst into their room and thunder at them: "Meet me in the dining room!"

Will and his brother left their beds and stepped warily into the room. They saw the uncle glaring at them menacingly. He clutched a wooden stick wrapped in duct tape. It was a weapon.

The uncle seemed to think that one of them had taken a snack without asking. There would be hell to pay.

The uncle smacked Will, and then reared back and swung so hard across his brother's ribs that the stick broke. He banged his brother's head against the wall and kicked him, again and again.

The beatings became nearly as routine as the daily chores, and the boys were eventually taken to a foster home.

Will was grateful that he and his brother were placed in the same home. "When you are sent to live with a stranger," he said, "it helps to be with someone you love and has shared your path."

He worried about his mother. She had grown up poor in a treacherous home. She had become pregnant after being raped as a teenager. Early in life, she took solace in alcohol and drugs, and then suffered its ravages. Throughout his childhood, Will would call his mom to check on her. She would usually tell her son that she was doing well and that she was clean. But he could often discern otherwise by the sound of her voice–scared, timid, and quite often, slurred.

Will, who had never met his father, sometimes wondered what exactly he had done to deserve all of the troubles. He grew distrustful. He was reluctant to engage other people. He skipped school.

"I was angry at the world," he explained. "So angry that I would punch anything in my way–people, walls, trees."

Sometimes, he would sprint one hundred yards along the school football field, then turn around and race back another one hundred yards, just to try to burn the negative energy and exhaust the overwhelming anger.

And then one day, the hurting young man turned to poetry. He titled one of his poems, "Trapped Doors."

It read:

> *I wrote a note to father time,*
> *Heal this broken heart of mine.*
> *No more pain, no more crying,*
> *Consumed by my pride, release me from these chains.*

Writing did not cure his woes, but it was cathartic. And while the process wasn't painless, it hurt less than punching a tree.

Haley Olsen remembered the good times. She and her parents, a younger sister, and the family's two dogs, were living in a modest but decent house in Cumberland County.

"Life was awesome," she said.

Her mom worked at a law farm. Her dad, who stood six feet, two inches tall and was powerfully built, was a housepainter. When Haley was eight years old, her dad fell fifteen feet from a ladder while working at a Chipotle restaurant. He suffered a fractured disk and other serious injuries. The doctors prescribed high-powered painkillers.

"He was like a walking zombie," Haley said.

The family moved to a crowded house – shared with her grandparents, an aunt, and cousins – and made their living quarters in the basement. Haley learned that her parents were selling some of the painkillers. If her parents tried to hide the activity from their daughter, it didn't work.

"As a kid, I knew the nicknames of all the drugs," she said.

They moved from one house to another. There were escalating arguments and accusations between the parents. Her dad's depression deepened and then he gave up hope.

When he tried unsuccessfully to hang himself, he was admitted to a psychiatric ward. Haley, then ten years old, discovered the suicide note. With her mother, she went to see him in the hospital. She brought him a gift, a copy of her favorite book, "Little Red Riding Hood." It had always brought her comfort. She thought it could do the same for her dad.

"I remember asking him, 'Why would you do this? Don't you love me? Don't you care?'"

"I have nothing to live for," he told her.

Through her tears, Haley pleaded, "You have me! Isn't that enough?"

He came home about a month later. He seemed better. But the family was on the move again, this time to a grungy place in a rough neighborhood. There were bullet holes in the building.

Haley developed bumps on her arms and legs. Her relentless scratching eventually caused scars. Her parents finally realized that she was being bitten by bedbugs.

Late one night, child authorities showed up at their home and confronted her with a list of questions:

"Do your parents hit you?"

"No," she replied, though she remembered thinking, "Only when I deserve it. I do a lot of stupid stuff, so I deserve to get smacked sometimes."

"Do your parents do drugs?"

"No, not bad drugs," she told them, explaining later, "I didn't see weed and pills as being really bad drugs."

Haley was in the sixth grade when she watched her father die. He was thirty-eight years old.

Not long after, Haley found dope bags and discovered her mom was shooting heroin. Haley and her sister were placed in a foster home. Once a week, her mother would be allowed to come for a short visit, except when she was in jail. When her mom cleaned up, the girls were allowed to go home.

Her mom's sobriety would not last. One afternoon, Haley was summoned to the school office. A child welfare authority was there waiting for her.

Haley squared off like a fighter and balled her fists, as tears streamed down her face.

Everything in her life seemed to be ruined by drugs.

Sitting in the offices of child services, with no idea where she would be going, Haley called her mother on the phone.

"I am so angry at you!" she told her mom. "But I love you."

She moved home when her mother stopped using heroin and went through treatment with methadone. Haley worked forty hours a week at McDonald's and daydreamed about a better life.

Before Anthony Hayes was placed in foster care, he was homeless and living on the streets with his parents, both of whom were strung out on heroin.

Despite the hardship he endured, and the decision by his parents to give him up to the state child welfare system, Anthony harbored no anger towards them. He even managed a measure of gratitude.

"I am thankful," he said, "that at least they *knew* they couldn't take care of me."

A slender teenager with close-cropped dark hair, Anthony looked younger than his age. With his striking intellect, however, he could have passed for a college student at the head of the class.

"A lot of my teachers say I'm gifted," he said, shrugging at the notion. "But I feel like anyone can do things if they just put their mind to it. I don't see that as gifted."

In the years since he was placed in foster care, he had never seen his father. He saw his mother once, on the street, but she did not recognize her son. She was standing outside a Walmart in Cumberland County. She was begging for change.

"She looked beaten up," recalled Anthony, who did not engage his mother, but simply said a prayer for her.

Anthony's foster guardian had some struggles of her own. The dark moods of the guardian sometimes left him fearful. (Anthony preferred the term *legal guardian* to foster parent, which he viewed as a euphemism for what tended to be a transient, transactional living arrangement.) When the guardian picked him up from his therapy session one day, she sat behind the steering wheel and grew increasingly agitated, seemingly without reason.

"She raised her hand in a fist," Anthony said. "I thought she was going to hit me."

Frightened, he stepped out of the car.

"Bye!" the woman said simply, and she zoomed away.

That was the last he saw her.

Left alone on the street, Anthony walked back into the therapist's office and asked if someone could call family services.

"You shouldn't just abandon somebody, you know," Anthony said.

Until the authorities could find someone who would take him, Anthony was placed in a residential group facility with nine other kids.

"It seemed hostile," Anthony said of the residential facility. "The people intimidated you. It wasn't maybe as bad as you'd think. But it was bad."

He was later placed with three other kids in a house with a man named Dexter who was in his late forties. Dexter recited the house rules: "Don't steal and don't go into anyone else's room. Bedtime is eight thirty every night."

"Dexter told me that if I'm good, I can stay there until I'm eighteen," Anthony said.

Each night, Anthony prayed for guidance and gave thanks for food, clothing, and a place to live. He also gave thanks for the First Star group, a family he could count on.

Desiree Isola didn't have many family memories from childhood.

"I just remember that my parents were always in their room doing drugs," she said.

Her grandmother, who knew the dangers in the home, grew especially worried about Desiree as the summer neared. At least in school, there were teachers and counselors to check on her well-being. At age ten, Desiree moved in with her grandma.

Stealing money for drugs, her father ultimately went to prison for armed robbery.

"He's done bad stuff, but he's not a bad person, and he's got a good heart," Desiree said. "I wrote him a letter. I feel better that he's in jail now. He's safe."

It had been more than six years since Desiree had talked to her mother.

"She could be lying in a hospital bed right now from an overdose of heroin," Desiree said, "and I wouldn't know it."

She had searched for her mom on Facebook. Desiree discovered she was living in Florida. Her mother hadn't told her she was leaving New Jersey. Desiree looked at the photo of her mother on the screen.

"She's too thin," she said, "and her teeth have rotted."

When I heard about First Star and its work, I went to meet Melissa. During our first meeting, I told her that if she could find one hundred kids who had an incarcerated parent or who had experienced foster care – and needed help for college – I would provide them full-ride scholarships. I was eager to establish a beta program with a large number of kids in a specific area to test out some new ideas and to challenge my belief that these kids were just as smart as the rest of us. Melissa would soon join our cause at Give Something Back.

"I can find you thirty kids right now," she said, overcome with emotion.

CHAPTER THREE

NOW I HAVE A CHANCE

For a few moments, the words didn't seem to register with the First Star foster kids of South Jersey.

A woman from the Give Back scholarship program, standing at the front of the classroom, had just made an announcement that seemed too good to be true:

We want to send you to college for free—no tuition, no cost for room and board, or fees.

Some of the students stared blankly. Others looked confused.

Anthony Hayes, with a furrowed brow, raised his hand and spoke up:

"Are you saying you're offering to give us a loan of about a million dollars?" he asked.

To these economically strapped kids, the idea of paying for college seemed so out of reach it might as well cost $1 million.

But this was no loan.

With a look of disbelief, Will Denson chimed in: "I'm going to college for free?"

The Give Back representative repeated the promise:

You're going to college for free.

"Thank you!" Will replied, as his eyes welled. "Thank you!"

The classroom erupted in cheers–and then tears.

The kids were told they could attend one of Give Back's partner colleges in New Jersey. If a student did not want to start at a four-year college, other options included a two-year community college or a trade school.

Here was the bargain: The students would be required to keep up their grades, take college prep courses, and stay out of trouble. If they worked hard, there would be a college slot waiting for them, paid in advance.

"This is a once-in-a-lifetime opportunity," Melissa told the kids. "You now have no obstacles but yourself. It's completely up to you. There's nothing standing between you and what you want to achieve in life. Nothing.

"From now on, every time you walk into a classroom," she said, "you should try harder, knowing the possibilities that lie ahead.

"The good news is that I know every one of you," she said. "And I know that you can do this. And we're going to do everything we can to get you there."

Her husband Wally stepped up. He asked the students to close their eyes for a few moments and try very hard to visualize reaching their academic goals.

"When you receive your diploma," he said, "you will stop and remember this magical moment here today."

Now the tears were falling hard. Students tried to muffle sobs. Some kids fell into the arms of a foster peer, or held hands tightly with someone nearby.

"I can't believe I'm actually going to college!" a girl cried out in a wavering, but triumphant voice. "It's just so hard to believe."

Another student talked of his "doubters," especially the "kids at school who thought I couldn't do it."

One girl said the scholarship offer empowered her to overcome the cruelty of an abuser in her childhood home who compared her to dirt.

"You can't hold me down anymore," she said, thinking of her tormentor.

Haley Olsen's mind raced to the future, a day when she would have a college degree, a thriving career, and the chance "to give my children the kind of life" that she had so keenly wished for herself.

"I always knew I wanted to go to college," she said. "I just didn't know how."

One after another, the kids rose to tell their stories.

"All of my life, I was told it was impossible," said one of the girls. "They said I'd end up like my mom. Now I have a chance."

With all the sobbing and crying, Anthony tried to bring a bit of comic relief amid the flood of tears.

"Hey, who brought the bowl of onions in here?" he asked.

The kids laughed. And they cheered once more, even louder than before.

"A lot of my family succumbed to a lot of bad things," one boy said, as heads nodded in understanding. "All of my life, I have told myself that I was going to accomplish something. I always had that stress on top of me – the fear that I would fall into this pit, with no way to get out."

He stopped for several moments, trying to stifle the sobs.

"It's okay to cry!" a young voice nearby called out in encouragement – and the boy continued to describe his journey:

"Something like this comes along, and all that stress gets relieved," he said. "When I walk up to get my diploma, I'm going to remember this moment and all the other moments with my family – and with *this* family here."

The First Star kids burst into roars of solidarity.

Joshua Meekins, a former Give Back scholar who graduated from Villanova University and came back to work for the organization, told the students he could understand if they were nervous, but that they would have plenty of support.

"We believe in you," he said. "Don't ever feel like you're doing this alone. Pick up a telephone and call or text. We're here for you."

The students looked at one another and smiled and shook their heads in disbelief. Will brushed tears from his cheeks with the back of his hand.

"We have people walk in and out of our lives," one girl said to her fellow foster kids. "It's good to have someone stay around for a while."

When I went to visit the First Star students, I made a simple request: "Don't screw this up for us."

They laughed. But I was serious.

I recognized their challenges. It can be difficult to keep test dates straight when you're not even sure where you'll be living next month. Being poor can make school difficult enough. When you have a lot of people living together in a small place, as I had experienced as a kid, it's tough just to find a quiet space to study. And there was the chance that turmoil could erupt at any moment. These were kids who knew exactly what I was talking about.

Plenty of them knew what it's like to muster the courage to forge ahead when you don't have support from parents. I told the kids that they had surely experienced hardship more severe than I had known, but that I knew my share about troubles in the house.

My own father, far from encouraging me to pursue higher education, had talked about how he hated college and loathed the "pointy-headed" elitists who supposedly thought they were better than we were. He was a bitter man who bragged that he had never read a book in his life.

My mother worked as a night shift waitress to help support us because my dad squandered his paycheck on drinking and chasing women. It's hard to believe, but I actually grew up dreaming and hoping that my father would abandon us.

I did my very best to convince my mom to leave him. She had more than enough reason, and I was willing to support her to pay the bills. She initially refused but eventually did just that. I hired my mom and two of my sisters to work in my fledgling business. This ended that nightmare.

When I escaped my dysfunctional household and went off to the University of Illinois, I told the kids, I finally felt free. I studied hard and worked a lot of hours as a dishwasher in food services. I earned a bachelor's degree in three years. In my fourth year, I earned a master's degree in computer science.

After I graduated, I worked for a while as a professor at a community college. And then I decided to go off on my own as an entrepreneur. I thought it wouldn't take long for me to get rich.

I was wrong.

For decades, I struggled mightily and experienced business setbacks and failures. Sometimes there wasn't enough money to keep up with the bills. I was faced with the threat of home foreclosure. I nearly lost my car to the "repo man" for being behind in my payments.

My hard work ultimately paid off. I succeeded beyond my wildest dreams.

When success came, I wondered what you do with your money when you have more than you need. I didn't want a yacht or another house. Fancy cars didn't hold any interest for me. Buying a jet airplane seemed ridiculous to me.

But I do feel good about trying to make a difference in the lives of young people who could benefit from a first chance to make a wonderful life. I believe in paying back.

When I had some extra money, I founded Give Something Back, a mentoring and scholarship program. It was a way of paying forward. Give Back is on track to put more than 1,500 kids through college. But at some point, I told these students, I'll run out of money.

So I founded a new company, Beyond, that would benefit the Give Back program. Profits from the business would hopefully generate money for a lot more scholarships for a very long time.

That still wouldn't be nearly enough to pay for college for everyone who has experienced foster care or the incarceration of a parent. It was my hope that the government will someday cover college costs for all of these kids. Scholarships seemed to me like a smarter investment than prisons.

And that's where I needed the help and hard work from these First Star foster kids–and other scholarship recipients like them. We needed to show that this scholarship program worked and could be replicated. If the kids didn't make it through college, and the program was viewed as a failure, nobody would want to adopt our model. I needed them to succeed to provide opportunities for all the other kids, like them, hoping for a better life.

I proudly talked about the track record of the Give Back program. We had achieved a college graduation rate of 90 percent. That's pretty amazing. And almost all of our students graduated in four years. They didn't take five or six years to finish, which had become commonplace–and very expensive.

I was blunt with the First Star students. There were some skeptics when Give Back started its outreach to kids like them–young people who have experienced foster care or the incarceration of a parent. The doubters questioned whether students from those backgrounds would be able to compete in the college classroom. They raised concerns about whether such kids could truly be "college material."

Those were fighting words to me. I was outraged by the idea that a tough background would disqualify students from an opportunity to reach academic success. Kids from your backgrounds, I told them, are as smart and capable as the best. If anything, you know more about the key to success. You've had to figure things out on your own. You have resilience and grit. And that's going to drive you to success.

Set your goals high, I told them. Don't settle for thinking a B average is good enough. You should set your mind on straight As. Every single one of you is capable of it.

One foster student shouted, "We're going to change the world!"

CHAPTER FOUR

THE DANGERS AT HOME

As a top prosecutor in San Bernardino County, Mary Ashley specialized in crimes against children. She knew by heart the details of horrifying cases that shook her to her core – kids who were starved, imprisoned, beaten, and raped.

In one shocking case, six children were forced to have sex with each of their siblings – the youngest was ten years old – as the parents watched in a form of sadistic entertainment. One of the children ended up in a mental institution.

In another case, a young boy was diagnosed with psychosocial dwarfism. He was physically and mentally years behind his peers – because he had been forced to live in captivity, like a caged animal, and did not develop properly. He was given a bowl of water for drinking and a pail for emptying his bladder and bowels. Routinely beaten, his body was covered in scars.

Mary told me I really ought to think about helping the kids of San Bernardino County. It was impoverished, one of the poorest counties in California. The crime rate was high. The network of child services was strained by extremely high demand. And it was the home of a large college, California State University, San Bernardino, which could be a helpful resource and a possible fit among the partner schools in the Give Back program.

Mary worked with Dr. Amy Young, a physician who specialized in pediatric forensics—in other words, a child abuse doctor.

While still in medical school, Amy and her husband, Justin, had decided to adopt a baby from the foster care system, an infant girl with serious medical problems that would require many surgeries.

"Everyone said I was crazy," Amy remembered. "They were like: 'You're heading into residency and you're going to adopt a child? A child with special health needs?'"

She had yet to finish her fourth year of medical school, let alone begin the harrowing marathon of residency. She and Justin were broke. They scraped along week to week, living on student loans. Justin worked at a low-wage job at a Home Depot and attended school part-time, studying for a bachelor's degree. To anyone with a lick of common sense, they were told, this was foolhardy.

She understood the reaction. But the others had not looked into the sweet face of this baby, a little girl alone in the world, a ward of the state with an uncertain, and quite likely, rocky and unstable life ahead of her.

"You can't save the world," people told the medical student.

Maybe not, she thought, but I *can* save this little girl.

She and Justin rescued the baby, Hanna. They adopted her and took her home. And before long, Amy gave birth to a son, Noah, a younger brother for Hanna.

When she became a doctor, Dr. Amy Young dedicated herself to helping children who had been abused and neglected. She became a forensic pediatrician. The demand for child abuse doctors like her could overwhelm the system.

In San Bernardino County alone, child protective services received more than 60,000 calls each year about suspected neglect or abuse. More than 6,000 children in the county lived in foster care. For some kids, help arrived too late. Loma Linda reported that twelve to fifteen children each year were brought to the medical center with injuries from abuse that caused death.

In serious cases of suspected neglect or abuse, the authorities referred kids to the Children's Assessment Center in San Bernardino, where Dr. Young served as medical director, working alongside social workers, therapists, experts on sexual assault, physicians in training, and others.

The walls inside were decorated with colorful pieces of children's artwork. A big sheepdog, Mack, who went home at night with the doctor, roamed the halls and let kids wrap their arms around him for comfort and companionship.

The center was designed to be kid-friendly, an environment that was less traumatic than the places where children were often questioned—a police station, the emergency room, the front yard with neighbors gawking, as a parent is hauled away in handcuffs.

Amy diagnosed children who had suffered bruises, burns, rib fractures, abdominal injuries, and brain damage. She cared for a ten-year-old girl who was pregnant by her mother's boyfriend.

For all the talk about "stranger danger," she said, it was most often a person known to a child who was responsible for sexual attacks and other forms of abuse.

In cases of sexual assault, she explained, the abuse had usually been long-running. A perpetrator often started by grooming a targeted victim—paying special attention, giving compliments, or buying gifts. And then he started to bargain with the child.

"He might say, 'I do things for you—like buy you shoes—so you should do something for me,'" she said, adding that the abuse was often accompanied by threats. "'If you tell anybody, I'll hurt your mother.'"

These cases were often very difficult to assess. Very young children cannot verbalize, while older children were often reluctant to speak the awful truth.

"The child might not want to get anyone in trouble," the physician explained. "They know that speaking up can cause changes in the family. The abuser might be the moneymaker. And siblings can get angry at the kid who discloses the abuse."

These children often live with secrets—and some surely go a lifetime without uttering a word.

"If everyone likes him," she said young people wondered, "who is going to believe me?"

There were good reasons for a child to fear being blamed. In many cases, Dr. Young had seen parents take the side of a partner suspected of abuse and denounce the child as a liar who "makes things up all the time" and cannot be trusted. In cases of breaking up the household, it was not uncommon for a parent to choose a romantic partner over a child, even if that meant abandoning a son or daughter to the child welfare authorities.

When she first entered the field, Dr. Young said she assumed that removing the children from abusive environments—and placing them in foster care—meant the problem was solved. The foster home, she took for granted, would be the "dependable, safe place" for a child who had been victimized.

"I was in la-la land," she confessed.

Not all foster parents had the best of intentions, she said. Some foster homes were nothing but short-term way stations, with neglectful or calloused guardians mostly interested in the monthly state stipend. In plenty of cases, a guardian would take in a half dozen or more children at a time, receiving about $1,000 for each child. In a lot of these cases, it seemed plain that foster care was little more than a for-profit business.

And there was certainly no guarantee that a child would be safe from abuse or molestation in a foster home. In plenty of cases, children were victims in more than one home. Abuse, whether in the biological home or the foster placement, could "change the whole trajectory of a child's life," said Dr. Young, citing greater likelihood of problems such as depression, cutting, unstable relationships, promiscuity, self-loathing.

"People look at women in prostitution and treat them like criminals," she said. "But the abuse typically started when the women were children."

Some of the foster parents, meanwhile, were naive. Foster kids could be quite challenging. Coming from a bad situation, these were children suddenly thrust into a home with unrelated strangers—a stressful, frightening, and traumatic experience. Not surprisingly, kids in these circumstances often acted out.

Exasperated foster parents, even well-meaning people, could be driven to wits' end by the behavior of troubled kids. In some cases, foster parents became angry and resorted to abuse, creating the same sort of circumstance that a child had just escaped. To be an effective foster parent, Dr. Young explained, it takes a lot of training, and they had rarely received it.

When I heard the stories from Dr. Young, with her expertise and her conviction to help kids who had lived through awful conditions, I wanted her to join our cause at Give Back.

I ultimately offered her the position of heading the California chapter for Give Back, helping to provide mentoring and college scholarships for kids who had endured extreme adversity.

"But I'm a doctor," she said. "How can I stop helping these babies?"

"I don't want you to stop helping those babies," I told her. "I just want you to help kids in Give Back, too."

Dr. Young agonized over the decision. She thought about the many kids she had helped liberate from abusive homes. She recognized these cases weren't always happily-ever-after stories. She knew the common reality of kids being passed among foster homes. She knew the dismal statistics about how few of them would go on to college and graduate.

But she also thought about all of the bright young children from troubled homes who could succeed if given support and a chance. It seemed an impossible task to take on such a big new responsibility. But that's what people thought when she adopted Hanna. And her little girl, given a chance, love and stability, had grown to become a thriving eighteen-year-old who was poring over her college choices.

"How can I *possibly* do this?" Amy thought to herself. "But how can I possibly *not* do this?"

She agreed to accept the post of executive director for Give Back in California. We searched for college partners in the state for our student scholars, and Give Back contributed $1 million each to Cal State San Bernardino, the University of La Verne, and Chapman University, in exchange for agreements to provide full-ride scholarships for our students.

Dr. Young, along with her staff, set out to find some of the hardworking kids in California who had endured extreme adversity and could use a break that would help them reach college – and ultimately – the commencement stage.

She traveled to Los Angeles to meet with one of these diamonds in the rough, a gifted and abused boy named Edwin Morales.

As far back as his memory could go, Edwin remembered being regularly beaten by his father in their apartment in a public housing project in South-Central Los Angeles.

In his mind, that was simply a common feature of life as a young child: Your dad, a mean-spirited man with breath that stank of booze, would beat the hell out of you for no reason at all. That was simply the price you paid for being a kid. Edwin's brothers, after all, got the same brutal treatment.

"I knew I hadn't done anything wrong," he said, "because I could see it was happening all around me."

Their mother, meanwhile, was unstable and verbally abusive. She screamed at Edwin with such vicious cruelty that he "would rather not repeat the words she used." She was ultimately diagnosed with bipolar depression.

When Edwin was in the sixth grade, an older brother was murdered. His mother's condition deteriorated so badly that she became virtually immobilized, unable to cook or clean. Edwin and his younger brother were left to fend for themselves.

Before long, the two boys and their mother were homeless. They bounced around the houses of friends and acquaintances. With no one paying much attention to him, Edwin started the school year a month late.

When their mother finally suffered a complete breakdown and was hospitalized, family services authorities intervened. Edwin did not know his mother or father's whereabouts.

In all honesty, he said, he was just relieved that they were gone.

Edwin spent a brief period with an older brother, and then was passed along to an older sister. With all of the moving around, including the homelessness, Edwin attended six different schools during his three years of middle school.

"I was lucky," he said with a shrug. "A lot of foster kids move many more times than that."

For a while, Edwin and his younger brother were placed in a foster group home dominated by loud voices, angry stares, hard punches. Some of the boys were hardened bullies. Edwin came away with visions of his little brother crying from being humiliated and beaten by those boys. When he could, Edwin would steal away to a nearby church, all by himself, looking for a place of peace.

Eventually, the boys ended up living with an older brother who cared for them as much as he could manage. Still a very young man himself, the older brother guided the boys through high school. Somehow, Edwin maintained all As and Bs.

"I was independent," he said, "because I knew I had to be."

In high school, Edwin joined the First Star chapter at the University of California in Los Angeles, a place of camaraderie for foster kids, with an emphasis on preparation for college.

Edwin received an email one day from a counselor at First Star. He was informed that someone wanted to take him to lunch and talk about his future. Her name was Dr. Amy Young.

"She was amazing," Edwin said. "I love Amy."

The feeling was mutual.

With guidance from Dr. Young and her colleagues in the San Bernardino office, Edwin pushed hard to get into a good college.

He went on to graduate from high school and enrolled at Chapman University, where he could more than hold his own academically with students who had come from stable, affluent backgrounds. He planned to major in business, with the goal of becoming an entrepreneur.

He was determined that nothing was going to stop him — not poverty, not the beatings, not homelessness, not the absence of parents.

Not even the cutting slurs he endured for being gay.

CHAPTER FIVE

BORN THIS WAY

Of the young people who experience homelessness in the United States each year, community services staff serving these youth estimate that an astonishing 20–34 percent identify as LGBT, according to a study by the Williams Institute of the UCLA School of Law.

"Given that we know LGBT youth make up about 8 percent of the general population of kids, research is clearly showing us" that these youth are "overrepresented in state child welfare, incarceration, social services, and housing instability," said Bianca Wilson, a senior scholar of public policy and an author of the report.

According to the Williams analysis, the staff at more than one hundred social service centers nationwide estimated that some 75 percent of their homeless young LGBT clients had experienced rejection related to sexual orientation or gender identity. More than 50 percent had been forced out by parents. At least 60 percent of these homeless youth, meanwhile, had faced physical harm or other kinds of abuse at home.

Gay kids were twice as likely to be placed in foster care, while transgender kids were nearly three times more likely than others to end up in foster care, the Williams Institute reported. LGBT foster children were also more likely than straight kids to be placed in institutional care, such as group homes, rather than with a foster family.

Youth advocates reported that LGBT kids were frequently rejected by foster families out of fear that they would influence or even "seduce" a biological child in the home. Religious views of homosexuality often played a role in the harsh treatment of gay children, in both biological and foster families.

According to a study by the Urban Institute of New York, homeless gay kids were also far more likely to engage in *survival sex* that involved relations with an older person in exchange for food and temporary shelter, an arrangement that frequently included alcohol and drugs. These activities would often lead to involvement in the juvenile justice system, where LGBT youths were disproportionately represented—and where they often faced further abuse.

Research by the Family Acceptance Project found that gay youth rejected by families were eight times more likely to have attempted suicide, nearly six times more likely to suffer depression, and more than three times more likely to have used alcohol and drugs and to have engaged in unprotected sex, when compared with LGBT young people who were accepted and embraced in their homes.

Overall, gay kids were five times more likely to have attempted suicide than their heterosexual peers, according to the Centers for Disease Control and Prevention.

"The unacceptable reality," according to a report by the Human Rights Campaign, "is that LGBT youth – after facing trauma and maltreatment from their families or caregivers – too often enter a foster care system that is ill-equipped to competently meet their needs and subjects them to further bias and discrimination."

Saeeda Johnson, a twenty-year-old barista and culinary student, was born into a strict religious family in Tampa, Florida. From a very early age, she had been fascinated with food.

"I love cooking because I like making people happy," she said.

As she put it, it was simply "part of who I am."

Something else was also part of who she was: her sexual attraction to girls.

Saeeda was in elementary school when she did something that horrified her parents.

"I kissed a neighborhood girl and they saw it," she said, "and they flipped out."

To punish her and keep her from straying, Saeeda was locked in the basement for long periods. Her mother insisted that she was not gay – that was unthinkable – but rather she had been temporarily overcome by a demon. Saeeda had been taught that homosexuality was such a heinous sin that it warranted death. The girl Saeeda kissed had also been raised in a strict religious home and had been taught the same.

"I would pray that I was straight," said Saeeda.

That didn't work. Neither did the beatings from her father, who was later incarcerated for other crimes.

"He would always say he was sorry afterwards," she said. "But I had lumps on my head and a busted nose."

When it became apparent that Saeeda was not going to "turn straight," she was turned over to the child welfare authorities and then placed in a series of foster homes.

"I have depression," she said. "I'd get attached to a family and then I'd have to leave. After a while, you're afraid to get attached to anyone."

Someday, she planned to show kids another way—an unconditional love and sense of permanent belonging. Unable to give birth as the result of a congenital medical issue, Saeeda said she wanted to eventually adopt children.

"I would teach my kids that we are all different in some ways," she said, "and that you shouldn't judge."

Despite feeling judged herself by others, including many in her religion, she stayed true to her identity.

"I'm still a member of my faith," she said. "And I'm still gay."

Shay House, a native of Oakland, was in the third grade when she was questioned by her foster mother about her sexuality. Maybe the woman had suspicions because Shay, strong and athletic, liked to play sports with the boys and routinely outperformed them. Perhaps it was a fear instilled by the brand of fundamentalist Christianity the family practiced. Or possibly it was a case of prescient intuition.

"Don't be gay," the foster mother would tell the girl over and over. "It's a sin."

Shay shared a bedroom with the biological daughter of the foster mom, and the woman grew worried that the young girls might become "too close." Shay, who later described the notion of a sexual relationship between her and the other little girl as preposterous, was nonetheless deemed too big a risk to keep in the house. She was shipped away.

California child welfare practice gave foster parents a seven-day option, a sort of easy "child return" policy. If guardians wanted to be rid of a foster daughter or son, they could simply call the authorities and the child would be removed within seven days.

The rejection of gay children, or those suspected of being gay, was well-known in child welfare circles. Christine Brown, a Give Back staffer who formerly worked in child protective services, recalled instances of prospective foster parents asking if a child was gay.

"If the answer was 'Yes,'" said Christine, "their reply was 'No.'"

Jessica Finkbiner, another Give Back colleague who formerly worked for a foster family agency, said being gay was frequently the cause for eviction.

"I don't want *that* in my house," Jessica said some foster parents would tell her. "I want a seven-day," they would tell her, referring to the removal of the child within a week.

Shay was painfully aware of the seven-day option. She would ultimately be placed in fifty-three foster homes, including eight institutional facilities. She attended twenty-three schools and eight high schools.

With brilliance, self-reliance, and determination, she would ultimately become an outstanding scholar at Mills College in Oakland. Shay did not claim that rejection for being gay was the culprit for all of her bouncing from place to place while growing up, or even most of it. But it was plainly the driving factor in more than a few cases.

As she entered her teens, she had never experienced a physical romantic liaison with anyone, but she had long known that she was attracted to females. She did not speak a word about it for fear that she would be judged, condemned, and forced to move yet again.

"I wanted normalcy," explained Shay. "I wanted stability. I wanted to stay in one place."

A striking, slender young woman who now stood five feet, eleven inches tall, Shay aroused suspicion among her peers as a teenager for not having a boyfriend.

At fifteen, she started to test the limits and reveal at least a bit of her identity. She attended a parade in San Francisco wearing a jean jacket, cargo shorts, and a tank top emblazoned with a white American flag. The outfit might not have triggered any sexual connotation among most straight people, but she knew that she was making an identity statement and sending a signal to people in the know.

"The aura of the look," she explained, "was pretty evident within the LGBT community."

Not long afterwards, a foster sister snatched away her cell phone and cruelly posted a message—impersonating Shay—announcing that she was coming out as gay. When Shay got the phone back, she eliminated the post, but not before it became the talk in the halls of her high school.

Her foster mother soon caught wind of the gossip and asked Shay if, in fact, she was gay.

"I denied it," said Shay.

"You can tell me," said the foster mother, seemingly showing sincere support.

"Yes," Shay said nervously. "I am."

A week later, Shay would be gone. Her foster mother had invoked the seven-day option.

"We're not going to tolerate that in this house," the woman snipped as Shay packed her belongings.

As Shay grew older and was sent to one foster home after another, she began to select clothes that were more "butch," styles associated with a more masculine look.

If it had been difficult to hide her true identity, honesty exacted a heavy price, too.

"I got really bad anxiety about the way people looked at the way I dressed," she said, "and I began to drink alcohol to relax and feel more comfortable with myself."

At age seventeen, Shay did a stint in a rehabilitation facility and learned that drinking, far from helping her boldly present herself to the world, was "keeping me from being the person I could be."

After treatment, sober and laser-focused on academic achievement, Shay entered her final high school, Sojourner Truth. She was the valedictorian.

She received a scholarship designated for foster kids, Together We Rise, and ultimately enrolled at Mills.

At the college, Shay won an internship for young entrepreneurs, writing a business report for a restaurant in New Jersey. During another summer, she interned for Senator Amy Klobuchar of Minnesota on Capitol Hill.

She spent a semester abroad at the University of Ghana – "the motherland," she said with a smile – but quickly learned she needed to watch her ways. In the clubs in Ghana, men could accept two *fems*, or feminine-style women, swinging together on the dance floor—indeed, they found it titillating—but they could not abide a woman dancer who was *mas*, or more masculine, as Shay herself identified. As a result, she rarely went to clubs and she did not date.

"It was only four months," she said with a shrug, "and I'm not a person who looks for pointless interactions anyway."

Shay became aware that gay people in Ghana were attacked and sometimes imprisoned. In some cases, she said, their mouths were filled with gasoline. Countless young gay people, meanwhile, had been kicked out by their families and wandered the streets homeless.

The experience deepened her desire to work on the plight of children driven from their homes and families. In the United States, she had connected with many gay foster kids, and they often shared experiences about being unwanted and denounced for being "impure."

"A lot of my friends ran away," she said. "Others internalized the messages and thought, 'Maybe I can change.'"

Back at Mills, she worked on her senior thesis on the impact of instability on foster kids, especially as it concerned education. Having been rejected so many times growing up, Shay was applying to thirteen graduate schools, including some of the most prestigious in the nation.

Her mother, who had neglected and abused Shay as a toddler and lost her to child welfare, caught up with Shay through Facebook. They agreed to meet. The mother, as it turned out, was simply looking for money. When she learned there was none, she called her daughter some obscene, familiar names.

Shay had learned by now to steel herself from being bullied. She was not going to take it from her birth mother. Resilient and brilliant, this proud young gay woman and foster system survivor was going to make a difference in the world, especially for the kids who were walking the path that she had journeyed.

She vowed: "I am not going to allow toxic energy to hold me back."

CHAPTER SIX

SCHOOL HALL GOSSIP

Mercedes was so crushed that she could barely talk about it.
She mostly stayed in her room with the door closed. She couldn't
stop crying.

Her mother had vanished to the streets. Nobody was quite
sure where she had gone.

Mercedes somehow found a way to blame herself.

"I feel guilty," she said. "My mom wanted to jump in with
two feet and have a mother-daughter relationship. Maybe if I had
tried harder. Maybe if I was nicer to her."

Mom Maw's depression grew worse. "I can't just stop all
communication with Angie," she said, her voice heavy with pain.
"I need to know that she's alive."

Mercedes, despite her tears, still needed to study for
final exams.

But when your mom is strung out on heroin and wandering with the wind, it is damned difficult to focus on lessons for physics or Spanish III.

At the high school, Mercedes froze when a classmate started talking about her mother.

"Your mom almost ran into our car last night," the girl said. "She was walking and weaving across the street."

A bunch of classmates stood within earshot.

It was one of the things Mercedes hated about life in a small town like Millville. Everyone knew your business. And people spread rumors whether they were true or not.

Worried about her mom and embarrassed by the gossip at school, Mercedes wanted to get away. When her mom was clean, Mercedes had posted about her recovery on Facebook because she was so proud. Now she felt mocked by her pride and hopes.

She skipped school on Monday, left early on Tuesday and Thursday, and came late on Friday.

She had been arguing a lot with her grandma. As Mercedes saw it, "Everything I do is kinda wrong."

She decided to stay for a few weeks at the home of a friend, Cassidy, but came home every night to check on her grandmother, and feed and walk the dog. One Sunday night, Mercedes started to doze off on the couch at Mom Maw's, and decided she would stay.

At about eleven o'clock at night, she was awakened by the noises of someone banging around the apartment. It was her mother, who was sky high on drugs.

"Her eyes were slits," Mercedes said. "She couldn't stand straight. She was making grunting noises."

Mercedes felt both helpless and outraged.

"I asked my grandma what she was doing here," Mercedes said. "And I started to cry into the sofa."

Her mom stumbled into the kitchen.

"I could hear her laughing," Mercedes said, "even though there was nothing to laugh about."

Mom Maw pushed Angie into a room, lay her down on the bed and told her to sleep, then closed the door.

In the morning, Mercedes dressed for school. She had barely slept. When she got to school, all she could think about was that her hopes seemed to have gone down the drain.

In Spanish class, she grew dizzy and disoriented. Her heart began to race. Her face was red and she felt hot. Her legs were shaking and her chest hurt.

She made her way to the nurse's station, where a cuff was put on her arm. Her blood pressure was high. She was told she was having a panic attack, but that if she could relax, she would be okay.

After a few moments, she left the nurse to go see her guidance counselor. She told her everything. The counselor listened patiently, but didn't have any magic advice.

"Keep your head up," she told Mercedes.

Mercedes dropped out of school in March.

She was too young to quit on her own, but her grandmother gave the school her consent as legal guardian.

The military recruiter told her she could get a GED, the general equivalency diploma, and join the Air Force over the summer.

"I got really depressed about my mom," Mercedes said. "And there's a lot of problems at school. Everyone knows everything about my home situation. And that's very awkward."

Mercedes also took umbrage that some teachers at school seemed to be pitying her.

"I missed an assignment and the teacher said, 'I know your home situation, so you can bring it later,'" Mercedes said. "I didn't like that. I didn't want to be treated any differently."

She had taken a job as a nanny for a couple with little kids. They lived in a nice house and the pay was decent.

Mercedes went shopping—not for herself—but for clothes and other essentials for her brother and a cousin.

"My aunt is struggling, and I'm doing really well," she said. "So I'm going to get one of her daughters an outfit and something for my brother Marcus, too."

Her mother was in jail again. Mercedes didn't know many of the details, other than her mom's sentence had been extended because she was giving tattoos to other women behind bars.

"I don't want to talk to her anymore," she said.

One recent day, a letter had arrived from jail.

Sorry I messed up, her mother wrote. *I'm gonna be a better mom. I promise.*

Mercedes shook her head in disbelief.

"I could find letters from jail from years ago," she said, "and they pretty much say the same thing."

Mercedes had gotten a call from her father. He apologized for being out of touch. It had been a year since they had last talked, and at least two years since she had seen him. He lived two miles from her, with his wife and a two-year-old boy.

When Mercedes went to Starbucks, the baristas noticed that she was wearing a nose stud and that her arm was newly tattooed. The ink spelled the word *ahuva*. It was Hebrew for beloved.

Mercedes's mind lately had been drifting to the idea of having children of her own.

"I really want to have kids," she said. "Just the thought of being able to take care of them. And I'd be really good at it. I would never put them through what I've been through."

She was about the same age as her mom had been when she got pregnant.

She didn't talk much anymore about her ambitions to become a journalist. The military was a respectable option. Even if she didn't stay for a career, she figured, experience in the military might help her get a job someday as a corrections officer. For people in Cumberland County without a college degree, working in the prison was one of the best jobs you could find.

Over the summer, the telephone rang for Mercedes. The voice on the other end identified himself as Domenic Merendino. He said he was from an organization called Give Something Back.

"I'd like you to think about going back to school," he told her. "Let's keep in touch."

CHAPTER SEVEN

I DESERVE TO BE HERE

———————— ⬥ ————————

"I know you have never met me," Kaitlyn Case wrote in a journal
for a young stranger, "but I believe in you."

On a crisp, sun-dappled autumn Sunday morning, Kaitlyn
and other First Star foster kids—all of them recipients of a Give
Back college scholarship—were assembling "kindness packages"
to be distributed to much younger foster children.

The packages included necessities that most kids would
take for granted, like book bags, school supplies, comforters,
and hygiene kits, as well as journals inscribed with encouraging
messages from the older foster kids who had walked in
their shoes.

The older students were writing and assembling the packages
in a colorful brick courtyard outside of a North Philadelphia café
with a whimsical name, the Monkey and the Elephant.

When they heard an excited voice call out, the First Star kids looked up from their work. Out of the restaurant charged a woman in her twenties, wearing a T-shirt emblazoned with the words *Foster Care*, and she issued a rousing welcome of solidarity to kindred souls.

"I was a foster child, and I'm proudly wearing a foster care T-shirt because *I now know* it's not a stigma," she proclaimed, urging the First Star students to shed any feelings of shame or embarrassment for their ward-of-the-state status.

"I know that I deserve to be here just as much as anyone else," she said. "I hope you all feel that way, too."

Smiles danced across the faces of many of the First Star kids. They were familiar with the skeptical way society tended to view young people like them, as if they were damaged goods. Most hurtful of all, some of the messages had come from their homes, both biological and foster.

In the journals, the older students wrote how they shared so many of the challenges and questions now confronting the younger kids. Despite the hardships, the older kids—now college-bound—were living proof it was possible to make it. The younger kids, who were given the journals, read messages that they could survive and thrive, too.

Kaitlyn wrote in the journal to a young foster child:

> *I am sixteen years old. I live in New Jersey and I want*
> *to be a lawyer when I grow up. When I was your age,*
> *people told me that I was stupid and I couldn't do anything*
> *good with myself.*
>
> *Know that you aren't worthless or insignificant.*
> *You are very special to me. Being in foster care taught*
> *me that only the strongest people go through the hardest*
> *situations. I need you to promise me one thing. That you*
> *will NEVER GIVE UP. Always follow your dreams.*
> *You have a purpose. I love you. If you ever need anyone*
> *to talk to...*

Kaitlyn wrote down her email address.

> *No matter where I am, whatever time of night it is,*
> *I will always be there for you.*

A parade of small foster children arrived to accept their kindness packages, some of them unsure why they were deserving of such gifts. In more than a few cases, the little ones were so shy they kept their lips buttoned and they stared at their shoes.

Will Denson, whose journal entry touched on the loneliness, uncertainty, and anger that young foster children are bound to feel, spotted a little girl who looked a little downhearted. He introduced himself, then gave her a big hug. Her little arms squeezed back tightly.

The Monkey and the Elephant was a fitting place for the older foster kids to reach out to the younger kids. It was a hip little café, with exposed ductwork, raw brick and hardwood floors, artwork on the walls, and rhythm and blues on the speakers. But it was most distinctive for its unusual hiring practice: it only employed people who had been in foster care.

One of them was Ruby Morales, who was proud of her recent promotion from barista to baker. A year out of high school, she was working to save money for community college.

It had been a hard road to get here. When Ruby was nine, she had been sent to live with an aunt after her mother died. She had been living there only months when a squad car came to the house and whisked Ruby away to a police station.

"I felt like I had done something wrong," she said. "I was being taken away by the police. When you're little, you think that means you're a bad person."

She was told that her aunt no long wanted to care for her. The girl had been raped in the house by a family friend. When the incident came to light, her aunt said she didn't want the girl in her home any longer.

"She blamed it on me, like it was my fault," said Morales. "She acted like I was 'looking for it.' *I was nine years old.*"

The police and family services authorities told the girl they would find another family member to take her. None were willing.

She landed in a foster home with a woman and three other children. It was a surreal experience – living in a house with strangers so soon after experiencing the death of her mother and the horrifying sexual assault by a man – an attack that was incomprehensibly blamed on the little girl herself.

At her new school, she kept it a secret that she was a foster child. She assumed that it was another cause for shame.

A dedicated caseworker kept an eye on her. Now and then, she would take her to McDonald's and the girl would open up about her experiences. Years later, the caseworker adopted Morales.

The former foster kids at the Monkey and the Elephant typically ranged in age from nineteen to twenty-two. The starting pay was nine dollars an hour plus tips. Each employee received a pass for the transit system as well as a meal during each shift at work. While working as a barista or muffin maker, they also received one-on-one guidance on personal finance, housing, professional and social networking, and employability.

This business with a social purpose was the brainchild of Lisa Miccolis, who had traveled to South Africa after college and encountered the problem of young people aging out of social services. It was similar to the predicament facing foster children in this country who find themselves on their own after reaching legal age. When a deadline arrives, state payments elapse for the guardians and the young people are gently – or not so gently – pushed out of the nest.

While the law might regard a person as fully self-supporting when he or she reaches eighteen or twenty-one – different states set various ages – most anyone who has raised a child knows well that the growing-up process does not typically conclude quite so quickly. Young people need advice. They need guidance. They frequently need a few bucks. And that is to say nothing of simply needing a place to go for Thanksgiving or Christmas.

"Somehow," said Miccolis, shaking her head in disbelief, "you're expected to survive all on your own."

While working in South Africa, she had befriended a sixteen-year-old boy who faced the prospect of being cut from social services. He had mentioned once that his favorite animal was the elephant. She told him that her favorite was the monkey. That would become the inspiration for the name of the café, as well as the symbol of her mission to help young people adjust from foster care to living on their own.

One of the café graduates moved on to study at Temple University toward a position as a physician's assistant. One became an outreach coordinator for a homeless advocacy group. Still another found a good job with a catering company.

In the hiring process, no background checks were conducted to make certain the job applicants had really spent time in foster care.

"We take them at their word," Miccolis said. "If they're making it up that they were a foster child, then they probably really need this program."

Inside the Monkey and the Elephant, an ebullient, thirtyish woman named Sharayna Taylor acted as program director, and when business was busy, stepped behind the counter to serve an occasional latte or cortado. She was a foster child herself who had experienced the slap of reality that comes with aging out of the system.

"I turned twenty-one and I literally never heard from my social worker again," said Taylor, whose mother, a schizophrenic, spent most of her life in and out of mental hospitals and jail. "You might be legally an adult at that age, but it's not like your family has somehow been magically repaired. It's still broken."

Taylor attended Penn State, where she earned a bachelor's degree in communications. On breaks, when other students would go home to see their families, she would board in various homes.

As a mentor to the younger workers at the Monkey and the Elephant, she shared her experiences as a foster child, including incidents that made it a challenge to preserve one's dignity.

"I lived in one home where they had installed video cameras to watch my brother and me," she said. "It was awful. It was so disheartening. It made you feel like you were in captivity."

There was even a lock on the refrigerator.

"You feel guilty," she said. "Did I do something to make her look at me like this? You get paranoid and operate in a way that makes you look guilty. When I was around the camera, I found myself acting very measured and unnatural. I wondered what my previous foster parent might have said to make her suspicious of me. Now I realize it was just her perception of foster kids."

Whatever the hardships, Taylor insisted to younger workers that there was no excuse for giving up or failing.

"I tell them my stories and they look at me and think, 'She's working, she's got a car, she looks like she turned out okay.'"

At the café, Taylor was on the lookout for occasions to praise the young workers. "Foster kids," she explained, "are rarely told they are good at things."

More often, they are told what they are doing wrong. And a message is conveyed, in subtle or blunt ways: They are expected to fail—to drop out of high school, become homeless, fall prey to addiction, go to jail.

But it didn't have to be that way.

"I never thought of myself as anything *less*, and neither should you," she would tell them. "I've seen people who didn't grow up in foster care and they're just as screwed up as anyone. The truth is, we all have the ability to be screwed up—and we all have the ability to succeed.

"You are a brand," she told the younger employees. "You have to build yourself up so people will invest in you."

While foster kids needed understanding and encouragement, Taylor said, it was counterproductive—and patronizing—to treat them with pity or to regard them with lowered expectations. These young people needed guidance and leadership, she said, not a sort of fawning sympathy.

"There's this look some people get when they find out you were a foster child," she said. "They act differently. They might lump you in with juvenile delinquents or the so-called at-risk population. Or they become very overprotective and treat you like you're breakable. People who have been in foster care pick up on that. And it can lead to manipulation, which a lot of them have learned as a survival skill in the system."

Taylor's approach to her younger charges was to set high expectations, and instill the understanding that they were capable of great achievement, despite their troubled family backgrounds.

She had seen reason for hope, as well as disappointment, in her own family. One of her brothers was homeless. Another brother earned a doctorate degree.

Some people described Taylor herself as a success, but she has shrugged it off. She believed their measuring stick for success was "the low bar used for people like me," who have grown up in foster care and weren't expected to accomplish much. She would go only so far as to consider herself "a *potential* success."

It has been her credo to make it on her own, and not as a charity case. Even when she was without a permanent home and was staying with friends and acquaintances, she never considered herself a couch surfer because she always paid for her stay, even when her hosts did not want to take any money. That way, she said, she qualified as a self-supporting tenant.

She acknowledged that her resistance to offers of help –
"I can handle things myself" – had sometimes led to a silly
stubbornness.

When her younger brother, Emmanuel, who holds a PhD in
engineering, would offer to carry her bags, she would rebuff him.

Emmanuel would roll his eyes at his headstrong big sister
and tell her, "Oh, knock it off."

Reluctantly, she learned to accept his offer and grudgingly
hand over the bags.

"I'm getting better," she said with a smile. "But he's probably
the only one who can get away with that."

CHAPTER EIGHT

A BRIEF KISS

On the glorious day of her graduation from Illinois State
University, Amiee Carlson, a longtime foster child and
the daughter of a mom in prison for life, stood tall in her
commencement gown.

On the top of her tasseled cap, she had printed these words
of triumph in glitter:

I BEAT THE ODDS!!!

More than a decade earlier, on the morning of her ninth
birthday, Amiee had woken and asked, "Where's Mom?"

While the little girl had been sleeping, a unit of police
officers, guns drawn, had arrested her drug-addicted mother
and taken her away.

With her mother addicted to opiates, Amiee's grandfather had become her primary caretaker. As his health declined, she was placed in a series of foster homes. One of them was a residential facility—an institutionalized group home where she lived in a frightening environment—"...the fighting, the stealing, the biting."

As a teenager, Amiee was shuffled around to four high schools in four years. She was never in one place long enough to fit socially or form lasting friendships. Other students kept a distance. They thought her clothes were odd. And she was guarded in her demeanor.

Amiee had reason to be wary. There had been so much disorder, so many broken promises. She had come to believe that the only thing in life that truly mattered was trust.

"When I tell someone I trust them," she explained in a coffee shop one afternoon, "that means more to me than saying, 'I love you.'"

During the eighth grade, she had grown close to one classmate. But the friendship would end in a hurtful betrayal. Her "friend" had surfed the Internet in search of a prison mug shot, and then posted it for the amusement of the other students.

The mug shot was Amiee's mother.

"When people grow up in a normal family," Amiee said, "they don't understand what it's like when your mom is in prison."

Children of incarcerated parents cope with shame, stigma, and silence. They often hide the truth or risk being ostracized. They tend to live with anger or resentment toward a missing mother or father. Some blame themselves.

If I were a better kid, maybe none of this would have happened.

Even the well-intended rituals of school life can carry a mocking echo. As a junior in high school, Amiee had been nominated by the school psychologist as one of the Students of the Month, an honor that included a breakfast with other selected classmates.

On the special day, Amiee walked into the reception and noticed that every other student was accompanied by a mom. She didn't fit or feel like she belonged. It was evidence of her flawed background, as clear as if the school public address speaker had blared: "Amiee Carlson's mom isn't here BECAUSE SHE IS IN PRISON!"

With a flush of humiliation, she ran to the girl's restroom and hid in a stall. She wept until the celebratory breakfast and program had ended, then dried her tears and made her way to first hour.

"When I was little, I never thought I'd go to college," Amiee said, without a hint of self-pity. "People with my background don't go to college."

As she looked out across the commencement audience at the Redbird Arena at Illinois State, she saw professors who knew about Amiee's remarkable journey and had come to show their admiration, and share her joy. There were friends and coworkers as well as some relatives, both family and foster. There was a volunteer from the child advocate organization, CASA, who had stuck by Amiee even after she had aged out of the system.

Amiee had worked two and sometimes three jobs at a time during college, logging forty to fifty hours a week, in addition to attending her classes and keeping up with her studies.

She even served an internship at the juvenile unit of McLean County Jail, where she tried to buoy the spirits of troubled kids. She told them that they weren't bad kids, but had been "dealt a bad hand." She told them that she had experienced hardships herself, but was determined to make it. They could make it, too.

At the commencement ceremony, Amiee grew so anxious to receive her diploma that she unwittingly jumped ahead of her place in line, and then had to turn back until it was time to retrace her steps across the stage. Despite the little mishap, she was feeling proud enough that she could laugh at herself. And then, after waiting her turn, she finally stepped up to clutch her precious prize.

Her supporters in the bleachers clapped loudly and proudly, and then paraded to Amiee's apartment for an open house. It was billed as a "Thanksgiving," as the new graduate called it, because the party symbolized her gratitude to everyone who had helped her along the way.

She gave special thanks for her late grandpa who died when she was eleven. "I promised long ago," she said, "that I was not going to let him down."

At the graduation party—which Amiee paid for herself—guests were treated to a modest feast of sub sandwiches, chips, soda pop, and a little bit of Champagne and orange juice for a celebratory mimosa.

The success of Amiee—and others like her—underscored that no one should ever write off kids who have been placed in foster care or who have endured the incarceration of a parent. Her experience also demonstrated the profound difference that can be made by people who care and help.

These are young people who have intelligence, tenacity, and uncommon perspective. Indeed, those who have faced adversities can become especially gifted in creativity, determination, and survival skills. Given a chance, kids with these coping skills can turn their tough experiences into an asset. They know some things that can never be fully understood by those who grew up with comfort and stability.

At age five or six, Amiee would watch helplessly as her mother would stick a needle in her arm, and then "shoot up and nod off."

It had started with a prescription for painkillers. There had been an injury. The doctor meant well. The drugs eased the pain. And the pills took her to a warm, comfortable, and euphoric state.

Like many who become addicted to opiates, her mom would eventually graduate to heroin.

She overdosed twice. She tried one stint in rehab, but was kicked out for sneaking drugs into the facility. When she would try to withdraw from drug use, she would often become so "dope sick" as she called it, that she became immobilized and irrational.

From her earliest memories, Amiee knew she could not count on her parents. They had separated when she was just months old. Her father, a hard drinker with a volatile temper, remained largely out of the picture. Her mom would sometimes disappear without explanation or bring around "boyfriends" who were really her drug dealers.

When Amiee was eight, and fully aware of her treacherous environment, she told her mother: "I want to go live with Grandpa. I feel like something bad is going to happen here."

A year later, after Amiee had moved in with him, her mother made a surprise visit one evening. It was late. She crawled into bed beside her daughter and confessed that she was in terrible trouble.

Before sunrise the next morning, her mother was arrested as an accessory to a serious, drug-related crime. After a trial that lasted a day and a half, her mom was sentenced to life in prison.

Her mother's prison sat along a road that meandered through a bleak countryside. Set behind cyclone fencing and razor wire, the correctional facility encompassed a series of drab, low-slung buildings.

This was no "work camp." She was placed in a barracks-style room, rows and rows of bunk beds, in what was euphemistically called a dorm.

The place was infested with cockroaches. The bugs were so thick that Amiee's mother would pull the bedsheet over her head at night and hide underneath. But she could still feel the roaches crawling across the thin fabric that draped her body.

Mice scurried through the kitchen and chewed into bread, leaving droppings on food. The kitchen workers were instructed to simply cut around the rodent excrement and serve the food to the inmates.

This was a facility that leaned more toward punishment than rehabilitation. But there was nothing about the conditions that hurt Amiee's mother as much as her sense of guilt. The world brooks little compassion for mothers gone wrong, a feeling that tends to be shared even by the mothers themselves.

She would regularly send mail to Amiee, and for years, the letters went unanswered. But she kept writing.

In the early years, Amiee felt no obligation to connect or empathize. Her mom's poor choices had left the child alone and delivered her to some awful times in foster care. It caused her embarrassment, pain, and a neverending sense of loss for not having a mom who was cheering on the sidelines at a soccer game, or taking her to the mall to shop for a dress.

Amiee did finally write to her mother, and the letter unleashed her bitterness.

Even though it hurt, her mom was grateful. The response meant her daughter was reading her letters. She was thinking about her.

It was as close to a sense of hope as she would know. Her daily existence was dreary. She had a job wheeling around a woman in a wheelchair. There was no pay. The prisoners had no access to the internet. If an inmate wanted to visit a doctor, it cost eight dollars.

As Amiee grew older, she thought more deeply about her mother's life. She was a woman who had never had an easy life. Now she was living in a cage, a person who had lost everything.

Amiee decided to let go of her anger.

When she turned sixteen, she decided to travel to the faraway prison – accompanied by her grandmother – to visit her mother.

Her mother, wearing blue prison garb, was led by guards into the cafeteria to meet her daughter. When she saw the little girl, who had grown into a beautiful young woman, she gasped.

"My baby," she cried out, as tears ran down her face. She put her arms around the girl and hugged her for the first time in eight years.

"I'm sorry," she told her daughter. "I'm sorry. I'm sorry. I'm sorry."

With her mother's arms around her, Amiee squeezed back tightly. She told her it was okay. She told her that she loved her.

Going to prison that day, Amiee said, was one of the best, most rewarding days of her life.

"My mom was clean!" she exulted. "She was authentic! I had never known her like that."

After Amiee graduated from college, she made plans to visit the prison again to see her mom, a woman who did not finish high school.

It would be only the sixth time that Amiee had been able to hug her mom in fifteen years. For two nights before the visit, Amiee could scarcely sleep because she was so excited. In her mind, it would be the real culmination of her commencement. The mother of the new graduate would finally be able to give her daughter a hug and kiss of congratulations. That would make it official.

On the appointed Saturday—weekends were the only time visits were permitted—Amiee arrived nearly two hours before the prison would open.

Visitation was scheduled to start at 9:00 a.m. But only if the authorities deemed it so. Maybe it would start thirty minutes later, or perhaps an hour or more. Or the prison might suddenly be declared to be on lockdown – the prisoners would not be allowed to step away from their bunks – and the visitors would be sent away.

On a warm day in September, family and friends stood outside the facility in a long line. Many of them, including Amiee, had traveled hundreds of miles. These were children, husbands, parents, friends. Some of the visitors wore pin-striped shirts and dress slacks. Others had the calloused hands of the working class. They were white, black, and brown. They were Catholic, Protestant, Jewish, Muslim, and atheist. They were Republican and Democrat, straight and gay.

But among the family and friends of the incarcerated, there were no superficial divisions. No matter the skin color, the cut of clothes or the size of a bank account, these were people who had shared common pain, worries, and want. Standing in a line outside a prison, no one puts on airs.

To get into the prison, Amiee needed to put any belongings, such as her license or car keys, into a clear plastic bag. A camera snapped a mug shot of each visitor. A guard patted everyone down and gave stern instructions: "You're allowed a brief kiss and a hug."

If anyone violated a rule, it was made clear, they would never be allowed to return.

The meeting space was a cinder block room with plastic chairs at plastic tables. Inmates and their guests were assigned to specific spots.

The room had the feel of a very old high school cafeteria, stripped of any sense of uplifting school spirit. A sign on the wall warned: *Zero Tolerance*. The closest thing to inspiration was a sign that carried a depressing undertone: *It's never too late to be who you could have been.*

Amiee sat across from her mother, their hands intertwined and their eyes filled with tears. At one side of them sat an incarcerated white-haired woman and her husband, both in their seventies. On the other side was a dad and his twenty-something daughter. Fresh-faced and lanky, the prisoner looked like she could have belonged to a college sorority just a few years ago.

Little kids raced around the room, stopping now and then to check in with Mom. For many of them, this was how weekends were routinely spent.

Amiee's mother gazed at her daughter, the college graduate, and told her how she had made her so proud. Fellow inmates, who had long been happily listening to the mom bragging about this brilliant kid, came around to extend their congratulations.

It was one of the happiest days for Amiee's mom. But she could not get past her sense of remorse, and likely never would.

"I am sorry," she told Amiee, a phrase she has repeated a thousand times in letters, phone calls, visits. "When you were little, you were so angry at me – and you had every right to be. I really messed up. It was the drugs. But now you're my biggest supporter."

As a kid, her mom had no easy time. Her own parents divorced when she was young. They lost their house, and she and her siblings and mother moved into a one-bedroom apartment in a sketchy neighborhood. There were five of them – and not a stick of furniture. At first, there was not even a bed.

A relative eventually gave them a narrow bed, and each family member would take a turn lying in the relative comfort of that bed for just a bit, before returning to the hard floor. A few years later, Amiee's mom lost her older brother in a fatal car crash.

As a teenager, she had become pregnant. She endured relationships where she was beaten. The drugs, for the most part, were medicine to numb the pain. And then the medicine became poison.

For Amiee's visit to the prison, her mom wanted so much to look as nice and well-groomed as possible. She found some peroxide and used it to make highlights in her hair.

For her part, Amiee wanted to pamper her mom. She went to the little cafeteria in the prison and bought her mom some treats—a cheeseburger, a plastic container of peaches, a Diet Coke, yogurt, a candy bar, and some instant coffee. And she paid for photos of the two of them together.

She told her mom about getting a call for a second interview for a job. The pay was decent and the work seemed interesting.

Her mom gazed at Amiee.

"I want to go home with you," she told her.

Amiee squeezed her mom's hands and fought back tears until she could fight them no longer.

Her mom came around the table to put an arm around her daughter. She whispered in her ear, "Pretty girl, are you going to be okay?"

Amiee slumped against her mom's shoulder, her body shuddering, tears spilling down her cheeks.

The clock ticked too fast. It was time for the visitation to end.

CHAPTER NINE

LOCKING UP THE MENTALLY ILL AND ADDICTED

Like many prisons throughout the nation, the Logan Correctional Center for women in Illinois was once a state mental hospital. In important ways, it remains a warehouse for the mentally ill.

Carolyn Gurski, as chief of women's division for the Illinois Department of Corrections, estimated that at least 25 percent of the female inmates suffered from serious mental health issues. Some federal studies showed that 75 percent of female prisoners had substance abuse or mental health problems.

"The state has closed almost all of its mental health facilities," said Gurski, "and we have become the primary provider of services."

It is a pattern that can be found in virtually every state.

By Gurski's estimate, a relatively small percentage of the women inmates had been convicted of a violent act. More than 50 percent of the women inmates were being jailed for drug offenses. A big share of the other charges included property offenses, burglary, and prostitution.

"The common denominator," she said, "is often that they were doing something to support their children."

And when the prison time has been served, Gurski said, "We usually give them a bus ticket for wherever they're going and say, 'Good luck.'"

In many cases, they are going to a homeless shelter. And getting back on track with a job can be almost impossible.

"Perhaps the most painful civil penalty that comes with a criminal record," wrote Amanda Johnson in the *Columbia Human Rights Law Review*, "is the long-term damage it inflicts on employment."

Dr. Norine Ashley, a psychologist at Logan, said women often face a much harsher reaction as compared to men, when reentering society after release from prison.

"It's just less acceptable for a female to be incarcerated," said Dr. Ashley. "There is the stigma of, 'How could a *mom* do that?'"

For some of the women serving time, the depression and other mental problems become too much to bear.

A hallway at Logan was reserved for women who had hurt themselves—including a woman who had clawed her eyes out—and others placed on suicide watch.

When counseling women who had tried to kill themselves, Dr. Ashley would ask why they wanted to end their lives.

"And they'll usually say something like, 'I'm just so tired,'" the psychologist said. "'I'm tired of being incarcerated.' 'I'm tired of having so much time to do.'"

Some states are trying to find ways to make life worth living for these women. At the women's prison in Decatur, Illinois, pregnant women and mothers with infants can qualify to live with their babies behind bars, provided their sentence ends within two years.

In other states, such as Oklahoma, judges give drug-addicted women the choice between prison or a demanding rehabilitation program.

Dusty and windswept, Oklahoma has long known struggle and hardship. This territory was the destination of displaced Native Americans forced to walk the brutal Trail of Tears. It was the home of the fabled Okies of *The Grapes of Wrath*, fleeing in hopes of a better life. In recent times, many Oklahomans have searched for escape and salvation in drugs. In some years, the state has registered the highest rate of prescription drug abuse in the nation.

Oklahoma jailed more women per capita than any other state in America. It incarcerated 151 women per 100,000. That was twice the national rate.

As in other states, the majority of incarcerated women in Oklahoma had been convicted of nonviolent crimes. And about 80 percent of the women behind bars in Oklahoma were mothers.

With the state's heritage of fire-and-brimstone religion, rugged frontier ethos, and oil rig laborers known as roughnecks, Oklahoma was not a state where politicians were eager to be seen as soft on much of anything, least of all lawbreakers.

"The district attorney is the most powerful player in the courtroom," observed Susan Sharp, the author of *Mean Lives, Mean Laws*. "And if they are trying to build a reputation of being tough on crime, they're basically going for the low-hanging fruit."

Despite Oklahoma's high overall percentage of female incarceration, Tulsa County stood apart in the state. It had witnessed a decline in the number of women behind bars over the past several years. The downward trend owed largely to a program called Women in Recovery, an intensive education, drug treatment, parental coaching, and job training program that was offered as an alternative to incarceration.

"They have a choice," said Mimi Tarrasch, the senior executive director of the program. "They can be here or in prison."

The program, funded largely by the George Kaiser Family Foundation, assessed the case of every woman booked in the Tulsa County Jail. For inmates who seemed a good fit for the program, legal advocates petitioned the court to delay sentencing while a woman went through rehab, which typically ran for twelve to eighteen months.

About 70 percent of the women jailed in Tulsa County reported having been harmed or neglected themselves in early childhood, Tarrasch said. They tended to struggle in school, often dropped out, and frequently became pregnant as teenagers. They came from homes with domestic abuse and likely saw it repeated in their adult lives.

Tarrasch noted that children of incarcerated mothers were two and a half times more likely to land in jail as compared to children of incarcerated fathers.

Women in Recovery was far more structured and intensely monitored than a traditional drug court or sober house. The women wore ankle bracelets and submitted to regular drug tests. They followed a dress code of business casual on Mondays through Thursdays, drawn from clothes donated by people in the Tulsa area. On Fridays, they were allowed to wear jeans.

A van picked them up from a dormitory at seven o'clock in the morning and returned them to their living quarters at six o'clock in the evening. As they progressed in the program, they took the municipal bus and began working at jobs in fast food restaurants, hotels, or factories. They generally earned eight or ten dollars an hour.

It was not unusual for a woman in the program to receive five hundred hours of individual and group therapy. If a woman did not have a high school diploma, which was often the case, she could complete the GED and take an online community college course.

The mothers took parenting classes and sessions on anger management, as well as skills to cope with stress-provoking issues, such as sibling rivalries. They were encouraged to tell their children they knew their actions had hurt them and that they had reason to be angry.

The program sought to reconnect mothers and children within a few weeks, if appropriate, and initially brought them together in a monitored playroom.

Amanda Tapp, who managed the parent and child division, said it was not uncommon to hear a small child beg, "Mommy, when do I get to live with you again?"

The women were encouraged to convey to the children that they were loved, that Mom had important issues to address, and that they hoped to see them again very soon.

The clients, as the women in the program were called, were taught how to walk into a child's classroom, something many of them had never done. They also built social skills, such as the appropriate way to shake hands and make eye contact.

The program helped the women secure state identification cards and find a medical provider. They did mock interviews for jobs. A finance expert gave classes on managing money and the perils of high-interest car loans.

The women took classes in yoga, Zumba, knitting, and the culinary arts. Supporters of the program took the women to art shows and ballet performances. The women also volunteered on weekends at dog kennels, food pantries, meals on wheels, and other service venues.

The goal was learning the duty and gratification of giving back. The service work built self-esteem and gave them something to put on their resumes. While they volunteered, moreover, they were working shoulder to shoulder with people in the community who might help connect them to prospective jobs.

When the women had progressed in the program sufficiently, they moved into apartments and reunited with their children. Even after they graduated from the program, they were offered addiction counseling for life.

Women in Recovery had a completion rate of 68 percent. If a woman failed a drug test or otherwise violated rules, the court and therapist were notified. The cost of the program ran about $20,000 per person a year, just a bit more than the state spent to house a prisoner.

"They come to us exhausted, traumatized, angry, skeptical, untrusting," said Tarrasch. "Along the way, you'll see a glint in the eye and hear a belly laugh, and we'll tell them, 'There you are! I see you!'"

One of Tia Pope's children told a Sunday school teacher that her mother was smoking something funny. As a lot of people in their community knew, Pope had already been arrested for drugs and done a stint behind bars.

The authorities were alerted, and before long the doorbell rang while Pope was playing with her children. Two male police officers and a woman from the child welfare authorities stood at the door.

They announced they would be searching the house. They found scales that were used for weighing illicit drugs to sell.

The authorities said that they would be removing her daughters, who were begging not to be taken from their mother.

"All I could hear was their screams, 'Mommy! Mommy!'"

She was arrested and taken to jail. She was told about the Women in Recovery program.

"I said I didn't want anything to do with it," she told them.

Her caseworker told her that if she didn't enter the program, her parental rights would be terminated.

"I said, 'Sign me up.'"

Pope had struggled with alcohol, methamphetamine, painkillers. She had started with sedatives at a very early age.

"When I was little, I was crying and throwing a fit, and my mom gave me a pill to calm me down," she said. "It was Valium. I was eleven."

In the women's recovery program, she had finally addressed some of her underlying emotional issues in family therapy.

"The kids struggle with being different from the other kids," Pope said. "I apologized to them. I told them that we were apart because I had made some bad choices."

The program arranged for Pope to get a job as a waitress at an IHOP restaurant. The therapy sessions were making a big difference for her and the kids, who stayed with an aunt.

"This program has given me more support," Pope said, "than I've had in my entire life."

In the depths of her addiction, Nicole Eddy would take her young daughter, Jillian, on "shoplifting" trips to Walmart. The mom stole food. She stole expensive light bulbs that could be returned for cash. She sometimes asked her daughter if there was anything that she could steal for her. It was sort of a treat for being a partner in crime. One time the little girl asked for earrings. So her mom pocketed a pair.

"Things spiraled totally out of control," said the mom. "I wasn't coming home. I was missing kids' birthdays."

The home became so unkempt that little Jillian missed long stretches of school because she had head lice. The girl missed so many days that she needed to repeat the first grade.

From as early as she could remember, Jillian knew that her mother was addicted to drugs. Her mom would go into the bedroom and lock the door, leaving the child wailing and banging on the door.

Her mother recalled that she once opened the door to find her daughter "standing there screaming, with a knife at her own throat."

Child authorities would eventually take away Jillian and a younger sister, Allison. Jillian stayed with her stepmother's parents, and later with her grandmother on her mom's side. Allison was placed in a homeless shelter, where she caught pneumonia.

When the mom was arrested for manufacturing meth, a judge told her she faced sixteen years to life. Or she could go to the Women in Recovery program.

Jillian remembers visiting her mother at the program. They would eat pizza, take a lot of pictures, and binge-watch the television program, *CSI*.

"It was the first time I had parented my kids sober," the mom said, and then paused before adding, in a small regret-filled voice, "or parented at all."

The younger daughter, Allison, who was only a toddler when her mother was arrested, seemed unaware even that Nicole was her mother during visits to the Women in Recovery.

"She'd look at me and think, 'Who is this lady?'" she said. "She would fall and hurt herself and not even look my way."

Little by little, as the mother recovered, both girls began to feel safer. When it was time to transition to semi-independent living quarters, the mom, now working as an administrative assistant, felt unsure if they should live with her. "I thought they deserved better."

But Jillian told her it was time for them to be together again.

"We got really close," Jillian said. "I wasn't scared anymore. I could tell her stuff. I could trust that she wasn't going to leave in the middle of the night. I knew that we'd have food. I knew that we were safe."

With her mom growing healthy, Jillian thrived at school. As a ninth grader, she was already thinking about colleges.

"She's a math genius," her mother said proudly.

Allison, too, grew close to a mom she once did not recognize.

"When Allison was four, she tripped on a coffee table, and she got up and ran to me and fell into my arms," said the mom, her voice catching. "I will never forget that day."

Clean for six years, the mom acknowledged she still experienced cravings for drugs.

"There are times out of nowhere that I'll think about it," she said. "And I have to use the skills I've learned in the program to cope. It's hard to explain to someone who has never experienced craving. It never goes away."

Lindsay McAteer was seven months pregnant when she was arrested for selling meth. Fortunately, she did not use the drug herself while she was pregnant. She said it was not for any virtuous reason, "but simply because it made me sick."

Her court case dragged on for more than a year. As soon as she bonded out of jail and delivered her baby, she went back to using meth. She even used meth on the morning she appeared before a judge.

McAteer was assigned to go to the Women in Recovery program, but was "still in total denial" and continued to use the drug.

On the day she was to start treatment in the program, she failed a drug test. She was sent to jail for eleven days.

"Sitting in jail, it was the first time I was sober and clear-minded in a long time," she said. "I was devastated. All I could think about was my child. When I heard him on the phone at my parents', I couldn't stop crying. I believed I was worthless. All I amounted to was guilt and shame."

Since McAteer finished her program at Women in Recovery, she started a job with a health association. She was also accepted to graduate school, studying for her master's degree in business administration.

As a way to give back, she led a twelve-step program at Women in Recovery. She also kept a picture on her phone of her lowest hours. It was a mug shot that showed her eyes vacant and drawn, nothing like the vibrant and engaged person she had become.

Her son, Talon, just past his fifth birthday, played with Legos and Power Rangers. He talked about his eagerness to start kindergarten.

He was unaware of the awful, scary times. He had no idea that he had almost lost his mother.

"He tells me, 'You're the best mommy ever!'" said McAteer, healthy and grateful.

CHAPTER TEN

FROM PRISON TO THE CORNER OFFICE

Samson Cirocco, an ambitious young account executive in
a Fortune 500 company, finished a quick business call with a
top vice president.

The VP was his mom, Michelle Cirocco, the chief of
marketing at a Phoenix company.

When Samson was a kid, telephone calls between the
two of them were often separated by a glass window. His mom,
a world before her VP days, had spent seven years in prison.
Samson remembers the day, as a little boy, when he was playing
Super Mario on Nintendo and heard a commotion outside. Then
he saw the flashing lights of a police squad car.

"Why are they taking Mommy away?" Samson asked his
father, Chris.

A few years before she was arrested for drug dealing, Michelle had divorced Chris. She took a job as a bartender, working nights and weekends, sometimes coming home at four o'clock in the morning, often with a buzz. Worried about the environment, Chris, who was a welder, came around regularly to check on Samson and an older brother, Zachary.

"I knew my life wasn't normal," Samson recalled. "There were all these people in the house, people I didn't know, coming and going at all hours."

The boys knew that drugs were at the heart of the trouble. Later, they would hear talk about counterfeiting. "Even now, I don't know all of it," said Samson, now in his mid-twenties.

A judge handed down a prison term for Michelle of seven to ten years. After the sentencing, she was taken to a cold, dark, dungeon-like room beneath the courtroom, once used as a morgue, where she shivered in cold and fear and waited to be transferred to a prison in Tucson.

"I was a broken person," she said. "All I could do was cry."

She was twenty-nine. Her boys were seven and four. The kids went to live with their dad at his apartment.

The legal troubles had been expensive. When housing was booming in Arizona, their dad found a way to recover from the financial hole, welding eighty hours a week. When he was putting in so much overtime, the boys spent a lot of time with an aunt. After the financial crisis and the housing collapse in 2008, which hit Phoenix especially hard, demand for welders dried up. For a time, there was a question about whether Samson would be able to afford to go to college when the time came.

His dad had been proud of the welding trade, but to survive financially, he turned to earning a living by cleaning swimming pools.

Samson knew it was not an easy transition. More than once, he told his dad, "You're a hero of mine."

Michelle and Chris had been junior high school sweethearts in Arizona. Both had dropped out of high school. Michelle's mother had died young. Her father took early retirement from teaching, joined Alcoholics Anonymous, and became a deacon in the Catholic church.

Chris had grown up in a poor and chaotic household with an absent father and a series of stepfathers. He was determined that his children would maintain a close relationship with both mother and father, and that neither divorce nor prison would break those bonds.

"Dad would wake us up at three or four o'clock in the morning on Saturday to drive us to the prison in Tucson to see mom," said Samson. And the next day, he would take the boys to their grandmother's and drive back to the prison by himself to see Michelle.

"My father didn't want the divorce," Samson said. "He was in love with my mother when she left him. And he never stopped loving her."

During the prison visits, Samson remembered attending parenting classes with her, as well as arts and crafts activities and board games. He remembered shooting hoops with his mother.

At school, some kids would ask, "Where is your mom?"

He told them she was at a camp, since that was what she called it.

Worried and confused about life, Samson withdrew as a grade-schooler. He became painfully shy, negative in his outlook, lacking in confidence. He would sometimes dissolve into tears.

"Weeks after I went to prison, Zachary was diagnosed with learning disabilities and Samson was afraid of his own shadow," Michelle said. "And I was so horribly guilty because I believed I had caused it."

Each evening, she would have a ten-minute talk with each of the boys on the telephone. She tried her best to build them up.

"She made me start each call with three things that were good that day," said Samson.

The habit never stopped. Every morning, he still wrote three to five things that made him grateful. At night, he wrote three to five things that went well that day.

Michelle tried to remain optimistic, too. She was assigned to a prison job, picking up trash alongside the highway between Nogales and Tucson under the blazing Arizona summer sun. In her last three years of incarceration, she heard about Televerde, a sales prospecting company that employed incarcerated women.

Televerde was founded in 1994 in a single-wide trailer, in the parking lot of the Arizona State Prison Complex near Phoenix. The call center started with eight incarcerated women as employees, working with rotary telephones and a phone book. The company would grow to employ almost seven hundred people. Nearly four hundred of these workers were incarcerated, and a big share of the other employees were formerly incarcerated. Some of Televerde's clients were Fortune 500 companies, such as Microsoft, Cisco, Adobe, and Oracle.

At Televerde's gleaming steel and glass headquarters, each conference room was named for a famous woman who had battled the odds: Rosa Parks and Susan B. Anthony, Mother Theresa and Helen Keller, Erin Brockovich and Harriet Tubman.

The incarcerated workers at Televerde were paid the federal minimum wage, far higher pay than for other prison jobs, such as working in the kitchen or washing the laundry. The money was put aside for the women in an account and given to them when they left prison. Samson's mother had built a sum of $25,000 by the time she was released.

The training and brighter work prospects for Televerde employees meant they were far less likely to stray into trouble. The average recidivism rate for former prisoners was about 70 percent. Among Televerde employees, it was 16 percent.

When Michelle was released from prison in 2002, she landed a job at the Televerde corporate office. She started at corporate just weeks after handing in her orange prison jumpsuit and being released from the barbed wire fortress of the Perryville prison near Phoenix.

When Michelle was nearing her release date, her sons and their father were counting down the days to her homecoming. At the time, Zachary was entering the ninth grade and Samson was going into sixth.

A lot had changed in those seven long years. Chris and Michelle had grown closer. They were determined to make a new start.

"Somewhere along the way," Michelle said, "we remembered why we had fallen in love in the first place, and we fell in love again."

They made plans to marry as soon after her release as possible.

As Samson put it, the day his mother was released from prison ranked among the three best days of his life, along with his wedding day and his college graduation.

"She walked out of the gate and she was bawling," he remembered. "We all hugged as a family and then we hugged individually."

By then, Samson recalled, "We were all crying like babies."

Chris and the boys gave her a bouquet of balloons as a celebration gift and the family walked together into a country field.

Michelle released the balloons, one by one, with words that sounded like prayers of thanks.

"This is for my husband who stood by me," she said through her tears, her voice shaking, as she released the first balloon to soar to the Arizona sky.

The second and third balloons were released for each of her sons. She sent a fourth balloon skyward for her late mother. A fifth balloon was released to the sky for those she had left behind the barbed wire. A sixth balloon rose in the name of family. And the last balloon sailed to the promise of a wondrous and triumphant future.

When they got in the car, Samson remembered feeling so happy that his heart raced. "When they were driving, I poked my head between the two of them," Samson said. "I was so glad our family was complete again. I felt like I finally had a family like everybody else does."

Michelle and Chris were married at City Hall three days after her release from prison. Eventually, they took the family and a crowd of employees—all of the invited women had spent time in prison—to celebrate in the Mexican resort town of Puerto Vallarta.

Michelle would go on to earn a bachelor's degree from the University of Phoenix and a master's in business administration from Arizona State University. Chris earned a bachelor's from the University of Phoenix. Samson earned a degree from Northern Arizona University and jumped on the fast track at Televerde. Zachary, meanwhile, went off to a brilliant career in the United States military, serving two distinguished terms in Afghanistan, and as Michelle put it, "he now wears a uniform covered in medals."

As a top executive at the company, Michelle occupied a spacious corner office with big windows that looked out on palm trees. As she zoomed upward in her career at Televerde, she bought a car to match her trajectory: a Lexus convertible. She and Chris moved into a stunning home in a beautiful Phoenix neighborhood.

She never forgot where she had been. "I am who I am," she said, "because I wore orange."

To stay grounded, she trained for marathons, volunteered her time, and offered up her battle-scarred wisdom to women in prison and others struggling at the Phoenix Rescue Mission. It was a way to give back.

"As a kid, I had fairy tale princess dreams," Michelle said, "and now I look at my children and my life with my husband and it has become so much more than I had ever dreamed."

But life was never just about balloons and luxury cars and romantic walks along the Mexican beach. Being caged in prison could be torturous. But learning to adjust again to freedom was not so easy, either.

On the day she left prison, she and her family went to a restaurant for breakfast. She found herself scurrying to the bathroom, fighting back tears of frustration over the sensory overload of choosing from so many items on the menu.

People in prison, after all, are told what to do and when to do it. They are not allowed to make many decisions. Soon after eating at the restaurant, she entered a mall and needed to rush out because she was overwhelmed by the whirl, the energy, the surplus of *all the things.*

When she first drove a car, she could not take the expressway—it was far too intimidating—but instead kept to the surface roads, driving thirty miles per hour, hunched with anxiety over the steering wheel.

Zachary acknowledged that he bore some scars, too, as well as plenty of ink. "I'm covered in tattoos from head to toe," he said.

The first tattoo read *Blessed*, and underneath was a broken glass that evolved to a whole, unbroken piece. It symbolized the healing of his family's life.

Three years older than Samson, he had more vivid memories of the day of his mother's arrest. He remembered being hustled into the back seat of his dad's white Ford Ranger with his little brother. His mother had asked if she could say goodbye before being taken away by the police. She kissed the window, leaving a smudge of lipstick.

"My dad never washed the window," said Zachary. "And every time Samson and I would get into the truck, we would kiss that window."

Growing up spending his weekends going to prison, Zachary missed out on a lot of social life. He remembered having a birthday party where almost no one came because he hadn't developed friendships.

"I'm now glad that I spent that time with her," he said. "But yeah, at times I was angry. I would go to school and hear about things I'd missed on weekends. I didn't blame my mom. It's just the way life was."

The embarrassment of a mom in prison, he said, also helped train him "to be a very good liar," a trait that he struggled to change until three or four years ago.

"I've never been able to make connections with people," he said. "I didn't know, 'Who is Zach? Who is he at his core?' It took me until I was about twenty-six to figure it out. But I believe that it's actually been good for me. I now have a level of confidence from going through the wringer."

Samson experienced a few hiccups, too. In his early adolescence, he had been a "complete straight edge," a kid who stayed away from anyone who smoked anything, and he avoided any place where there would be beer, a reaction to experiencing the pain that substance abuse could bring to a family.

In his last two years of high school, however, he was involved in some pranks, sneaking into the school at night, mixing it up with a boy who was a rival in romance, and partaking in some incidents of reckless drinking. When the police brought him home drunk, and his mother asked him why he had so much to drink, he unloaded on her.

"I said some really dark things to my mom," he said, still haunted with guilt by his words, even many years later. "I'm still a little closed off emotionally. I've worked hard at opening up. But because I've internalized so much, when I reach a point, I really blow."

But Samson was confident that the really bad old days were over for good. The family was financially secure, and most important of all, emotionally stable and committed to one another.

His dad, however, could not help but worry that things were too good to be true. He acknowledged that he was insecure. He owned a $500,000 house. He had a good marriage, a son who was a college graduate, and another who was successful in the military. But he still worried that he was just one bad decision from losing it all.

Chris explained: "I was raised with welfare. Every day, I came home knowing that something could be wrong and I'd have to put my things in a box—I actually had a box for my things—and leave on a moment's notice." He dropped out of high school, watched his welding career disappear, and didn't earn a college degree until he was forty-five.

"It's difficult for me to buy stuff and be relaxed about it," he said. "I don't feel comfortable with money. I don't care about cars. My kids have nicer cars than I do."

He added, "I know Michelle regrets a lot of what she did. And I regret a lot of what I did. But she could not be the person she is today without the humbling effect of what happened to her."

With a loving family and the troubles in the past, Michelle would remind Chris and her sons that they had something far more important than money.

A chalkboard hung in the house. On it, the words were written as a joyous reminder of the family's journey:

Happily ever after starts here.

CHAPTER ELEVEN

I COULD HELP YOU PAY THE RENT

Domenic Merendino of Give Back worried that Mercedes Marquez would drop out of school for good. He was determined to find better options for this teenage girl burdened by her mother's heroin addiction.

He phoned her and insisted there were better solutions for a bright, hard-working student than quitting school in the eleventh grade. Mercedes was grateful for the call and said she was open to ideas. For starters, Domenic arranged for Mercedes to meet with a mentor, someone who could give guidance, lend an ear, and offer a shoulder.

Domenic was a good man for Mercedes to have in her corner. Still in his mid-twenties, he had risen to the position of director of admissions and academic affairs at the Give Back office in New Jersey, even as he pursued a master's degree at the University of Pennsylvania.

But he grasped more than just an academic view of the chaotic world of troubled parents and their wounded children. He had lived it.

For as long as he could remember, his own mother had struggled with debilitating depression. When he left for school in the morning as a youngster, his mom would be lying on the couch. "And when I got home, she was still lying on the couch," he said.

Now and then, she would go out to the garage to smoke cigarettes or marijuana. He was in his teens when his parents divorced. He remembers they announced the separation on Easter Sunday. The next week, his father moved out of the house.

Domenic had been working since he was ten, dusting and stacking bottles at a liquor store run by his father and an aunt. His dad would eventually open a laundromat, where Domenic still pitched in to help.

His mother had met a boyfriend who introduced her to crack cocaine. When his parents split, she was left with the house, clear of debt, a two-unit rental property, an automobile, and $30,000 in cash.

"It's all gone," Domenic said.

There had been a stint in rehab in Michigan, and a stretch of staying clean, but the cloud of crisis never lifted. The boyfriend died and she later met another man, whom she married.

His mother and the man ended up living in a tiny, converted apartment in the back of a church—a church so small it had only about fifteen members in the congregation.

About every three months, his mom would text Domenic, pleading for money. One message read, similar to earlier messages:

> Domenic I hate to ask you this but we're in trouble. Jack's unemployment ran out and we have no money coming in at all. We will lose our car insurance and phone which we need when they call Jack back to work. I hate to ask you for help again, but we desperately need it. Jack has applied everywhere and no one is hiring him. Is there anything you can do to help. We're also running out of food soon…and I really need my meds. I'm so upset and I'm a nervous wreck.

In the beginning, Domenic would simply hand over some cash. That couldn't go on forever. Ultimately, he told her that he would give her money if she would agree to see a family advocate. She refused. Domenic, soft-hearted, gave her some money anyway, but told her that he had his own obligations and wouldn't be able to do much more.

Domenic had a pretty good idea of the pressures Mercedes was feeling. He knew that she worked a lot of hours after school and gave a good share of her paycheck to her grandmother. He also knew that Mercedes was young enough to believe that she could somehow save her mother from the ravages of heroin—and that she felt a responsibility to do so.

But whatever her mother and grandmother's problems, Domenic believed Mercedes needed to help herself. And for now, that meant earning a high school diploma.

Mercedes wanted to escape high school because the other kids in Millville knew too much about her family's circumstances and her mom's addiction: the public displays of staggering and incoherence, working the street corners to make money for a fix. It was scarcely a secret that she'd been locked up, again and again, in the county jail and the state prison.

Knowing that Mercedes struggled with the sense of shame around her classmates at Millville High School, Domenic explored possible paths to a diploma that wouldn't require her to go to the school. A GED would be one option, certainly a better one than simply dropping out.

Or perhaps he could find a way for her to take classes, online or in person, at Cumberland Community College in Bridgeton, not far from her home. Domenic picked up the telephone and found his way to Dr. Yves Salomon-Fernández, the president at Cumberland College. She listened to the story about Mercedes and gave a green light to the idea of the girl taking classes through the community college that would lead to a high school diploma.

Domenic called Mercedes to relay the option. She did not take him up on the offer. Instead, her reply made him even more pleased. She explained that she had decided to go back to Millville High and finish her senior year.

"That's even better!" Domenic exulted. "That's perfect!"

Mercedes's mom, Angie, had been released from jail on the day after her daughter's birthday. During this latest incarceration, Angie had written her letters, but Mercedes—disappointed so many times—had not responded.

During a visit to her aunt's house, Mercedes had an unexpected encounter with her mother. At the sight of her daughter, Angie started to cry. She walked over and hugged Mercedes. She asked how she had been and wished her a happy birthday.

"I thought I'd be really mad when I saw her," Mercedes said, "but I decided to give her another chance."

She hugged her mom back.

Her mother looked healthier. Her skin was clear and her eyes were focused. And she had gained some needed weight.

Angie soon got a job behind the counter at a convenience store called Express Mart and was earning ten dollars an hour. She started going to Narcotics Anonymous meetings every day.

"I'm trying really, really hard," she told Mercedes.

Mercedes told her to be careful about going to NA. Not everyone there would be clean. It was something she had learned at age six or seven when she would tag along to the meetings with her mother.

Her mom began texting Mercedes every morning to tell her that she loved her. And Mercedes texted every night to tell her the same. Her mother was staying with Aunt Julie, but Mercedes and her mom would spend time together almost every day.

Mercedes was awakened one morning by a ringing phone. It was Angie, anxious to hang out with her daughter.

"So, what are you doing?" her mother asked eagerly.

"Sleeping!" Mercedes responded with a groan. "It's eight o'clock on a Saturday morning and I'm seventeen!"

"Oh, oh, okay," her mom replied apologetically. "Go back to sleep!"

Mercedes was working a lot of hours at Aeropostale, a stylish clothing place she loved. She worked the cash register, but also rearranged the clothing ensembles on the walls.

"It's usually the manager's job," Mercedes explained proudly. "But she thinks I have a real flair for it."

She spent as much time as she could with her mom. On one outing, they went to Strathmere Beach near Ocean City, an easy drive from Millville, and just strolled along the shore and took pictures of the sandy hills.

Her mom started seeing a man. He seemed nice, hardworking, trustworthy—and sober. Mercedes was thrilled.

"He's her age and he has a job," Mercedes said. "He's the first boyfriend Mom's ever had who doesn't drink, take drugs, or smoke cigarettes."

If everything worked out, Mercedes mused, maybe she and her mom could get an apartment together. They could share chores, eat dinner together, stay up late watching movies, or just talk about whatever was on their minds.

"I could help you pay the rent," she told her mother.

When her mom accidentally broke a necklace that Mercedes had given her as a gift, she called her daughter in tears.

Mercedes was accustomed to giving financial help to her mom, grandma, and little brother. She went to Target and found the very same necklace and purchased it.

She walked to her aunt's place and found her mom on the front porch, still sobbing.

"What's wrong?" she asked her mom.

"I loved that necklace because you gave it to me," her mom explained.

Mercedes opened her hand to give the replacement necklace to her mother.

Now her mom cried even harder than before. She posted on Facebook: *Happiness is when your daughter shows up with the necklace you thought was gone forever.*

Feeling more optimistic about her mom's well-being, Mercedes started to think more about her own future. That's when she began to reconsider going back to high school.

Her Aunt Julie thought going back to school was a great idea. "You're not a quitter," she told her. "It would be good for you. And it would be good for some *other* people."

Mercedes knew that one of those other people her aunt was talking about was her mom. Her mother had told her that dropping out in the tenth grade, after getting pregnant, was one of her greatest regrets. Having a daughter earn a high school diploma would make her proud.

Her daughter going to college? That would be miraculous.

It made Mercedes nervous, but she decided she was going to do it. She was going to go back to high school. And then she would be headed to college – somewhere and somehow.

Mercedes also started keeping company with a boy who seemed nice. He was a student at Cumberland Community College. As a congratulatory gift for going back to school, he bought her a *Harry Potter* book.

She had gushed about Emma Watson, the actor who played the Hermione Granger character in the *Potter* film series. "I love her feminism," Mercedes said. "You know, everyone thinks feminism is about rights for women. But it actually just means equal rights for all."

Just the other day, Mercedes herself had opened the eyes of some boys who watched the way she could handle a basketball.

"Wow, that girl can shoot!" one of them exclaimed.

Mercedes just shrugged.

"It's basketball," she said, "not brain surgery."

Over the summer, she had read *The Color of Water*, a black man's tribute to his white mother. Mercedes herself was a mix of Latina and Anglo. She also pored over the *Millville News* and kept up with the latest on politics, pop culture, and national and international affairs. She was going to be a journalist, after all, so she needed to keep up with current events.

On the night before the first day of school, she called a friend, Jaida, and told her about her plans to return to the classroom. She also confided in Jaida about her worries that other kids would surely gossip and judge her home life.

"Who cares what anybody says!" said Jaida. "I am so happy. I missed you."

On some of the mornings before school, Mercedes was so filled with anxiety that she vomited. But she didn't give up. She excelled in the classroom and took a deliberate and purposeful approach to school and life. She made a conscious effort to dress sharply, replacing her old T-shirt and hoodie combo, because she believed a smarter attire put her in a more businesslike frame of mind.

She grew even more tender and generous with her grandmother. The two of them worked on giant puzzles and watched their beloved Philadelphia Eagles on television. She left Aeropostale, a place she adored, and took a job working behind the counter at McDonald's because she could get more hours and the pay was slightly higher.

The extra money meant she could contribute more to her grandmother, as well as treat her and her mom to occasional meals at the Millville Diner and the Chinese Buffet. She would shop for cool vintage clothes with her grandmother on Sundays, the day of the week when the price of items at Goodwill was reduced to a dollar.

"When I was younger, I didn't like buying clothes at Goodwill because I felt embarrassed," Mercedes said. "But now that I'm in high school, it's a cool place to shop."

Mercedes even worked on ignoring the snarky and negative comments of others.

"It used to be if someone said they didn't like the color of my shirt, I wouldn't wear it anymore," she said. "I'm trying not to be that way. And I think it's working. I'm a lot happier now. There is a plan. It's a good one. And there is structure in my life."

And then her mother, overwhelmed by the cravings, returned to the syringe.

When Mercedes texted her mother and urged her to go to a treatment program, her mom broke off communication for weeks. Her mother would reappear, asking for twenty dollars, or in the darkest moments, text Mercedes that she was going to commit suicide.

"I was freaking out," said Mercedes, who would skip class and go to the counselor's office for help. "The guidance counselor at school finally said, 'Look, you can't be in our office four days of the week.'"

At the end of Mercedes's first semester of her senior year of high school, Domenic, of Give Back, sent her an application for a college scholarship. If she were selected, she would be awarded a full ride to college – no cost for tuition or room and board. She could start a career without debt.

It would be the chance of a lifetime, the kind of lottery ticket that Mercedes had dreamed about. She would be the first in her family to go to college. And with the earning power of a degree, she would be the first in her family to escape poverty.

But now Mercedes wasn't so sure about college.

"I'd feel so guilty," she said. "I'd be at school, but my mom and grandma would still be here with their problems."

Melissa invited Mercedes to our Give Back office in Bridgeton, so she could mull things over. Domenic was there. And I was there, too.

She brought her latest report card, two As and two Bs. Her best subject was English. She was scoring a lofty 92 percent for her high school average.

To a high school girl, we must surely have seemed like grown-ups unfamiliar with the turmoil of teenage uncertainty, worry, and struggle. But in truth, we were all kids of hardship. And no matter how many years pass, some of those scars never completely fade.

Domenic talked to Mercedes about his own troubled mom and the challenge of moving on. "You shouldn't feel guilty," he told her. "It took a lot of time for me to realize that I can't be the responsible adult for everyone in my family. Now I do what I can, but I can't feel guilty anymore. I did for a long time, but I can't anymore."

Melissa talked about a period in her life when her own mother faced struggles. "Now I take care of her," Melissa said. "I pay her bills. I take care of her health care. But I had to go away and get an education to get the tools to be able to do those things for her."

Was Mercedes familiar with Rowan University?

She sighed and smiled.

"Oh, it's such a beautiful campus," Mercedes said. "You can study journalism there. And they have a soccer team. I used to play soccer."

Would Mercedes be willing to talk to a college admissions officer about the value of going to college?

Mercedes said she would listen. But her family needed help now. And her grandmother was leaning toward the military option.

One thing was certain: Mercedes did not want to let down the people who depended on her. She felt responsible to rescue them.

I told Mercedes that my father was an alcoholic and had been in jail at least twice. He had wanted me to join the Army. After I chose to go to college, he barely spoke to me.

There was nothing wrong with joining the military, I told her, but she shouldn't dismiss college. The average college graduate makes about $1 million more in a lifetime than someone who doesn't go to college. That was just the average. And I told Mercedes, "You're not average."

Mercedes smiled, but it was clear she felt as if she were carrying the weight of the world.

Again and again, she spoke of her feelings of guilt. She had some serious thinking to do.

CHAPTER TWELVE

REACH OUT

———●———

Some seventeen years ago, a pregnant inmate pleaded for
medical help. She said she was going into labor. But the prison
guards did not believe her and walked away.

That was how Christina Marie Colatriano came to be
born on the bare floor of a cell in the women's penitentiary in
North Carolina.

After her birth, Christina was promptly declared a ward
of the state. She was placed with an aunt in Delaware. When
she reached the age of six or seven, she began asking insistent
questions about why she was being kept from her mom. She
begged to see her. Eventually, a family member relented and
took her for an occasional trip to see her mother.

During those visits with her mom, who had been released
from prison, Christina learned more than a little girl should ever
need to know.

"I didn't want to think my mother was a bad person, so I ignored certain things," explained Christina, "like when she'd be shooting up in the other room while I was watching *Dora* on TV."

As Christina would later learn, her mother worked the streets for money to feed her drug habit.

"Nobody knows for sure who my father is," she said. She has a hunch it was a man named Jim, a sometimes-boyfriend of her mother.

"He was sweet," recalled Christina. "He'd let me sit on his lap and watch TV. I remember he wore a Flyers jersey. And he liked to make me laugh."

But she would not develop any kind of lasting relationship with the man who might or might not have been her father. Jim was deeply troubled. He ended his life by hanging himself.

In Christina's extended family, misery was born of the bottle, the vial, and the syringe. Much of the trouble seemed to be spurred by depression, which ran like wildfire among her brood. And then there were the secrets, more plentiful than answers, which made reality difficult to parse.

Despite the chaos, and perhaps as a result of it, Christina was driven from an early age to change her world. While other kids were playing outside, she would stay indoors and read books and solve math problems. If she didn't have homework, she would invent an assignment and complete it as diligently as if it were going to be graded.

"I was aware that my present wasn't good," she said, "but I knew that I could create my own future."

She kept to the wise course, and it paid dividends. At the end of her eighth-grade year, a letter arrived in the mail, informing her that she had been awarded a college scholarship by the Give Something Back program.

"I was ecstatic!" she said. "I cried. I was running all over the house. I was a little dramatic. But who wouldn't be?"

If she kept up her high marks and continued to demonstrate upstanding character, the Give Back committee informed her, she could attend the University of Delaware on a full-ride scholarship.

"The scholarship meant everything to me," she said. "I was already motivated. But this made me feel like I belonged and I deserved it and people could see it in me."

At Delcastle Technical High School in Wilmington, Delaware, she had completed her junior year at the top of her class. She was named to the National Honor Society and elected secretary of the student council. For her leadership skills, guidance counselors selected her to attend Girls State.

On the school newspaper, she was a prolific writer about the jazz band, sporting events, and just about everything else at school. In the drama club, she played numerous theatrical roles, including Mrs. Spoffingforsykes in *Heartburn Hotel*.

On top of all of that, she worked as a certified medic in the school nurse's office, making minimum wage, and she held a job as a cashier at a ShopRite store, logging about twenty-five hours a week during the school year and up to fifty hours a week during the summer.

For all of her accomplishments, Christina struggled at times with depression, the bane of the family. And then there were her worries about her mother, a woman she had not seen in a couple of years.

"I assume she's out there somewhere, probably roaming the streets of Wilmington," she said. "I do know that she's dying of AIDS and heroin."

Makayla Johnson, a year behind Christina in school, was also an exceedingly bright girl, a star scholar who was deeply reserved. She, too, had endured very painful struggles. These were things she seldom talked about with others.

Makayla had also been chosen as a Give Back scholar, and she and Christina became friendly enough to make small talk at school.

"We'd bump into each other in the hallway and trade compliments," said Christina. "Things like, 'Hey, I really like your shoes!'"

Christina could not have known that Makayla was also the daughter of an addicted mother, that she had been evicted with her mom from apartment after apartment, that she had been homeless, including once on Christmas Day, which was also Makayla's birthday. Christina did not know that Makayla's mom had robbed a store for drug money and that the police had kicked in the door of their apartment after the robbery and burst into the bathroom, guns drawn, to find a terrified eleven-year-old girl.

"Makayla didn't talk much about her upbringing," said Christina. "I didn't want to push too much because I knew it was emotional for her. She was often going through a kind of depression."

There was something else she did not know: Christina and Makayla were second cousins.

It was not until a ceremony for the National Honor Society—both girls were inducted as members—that Christina's aunt pointed in the direction of Makayla and whispered the surprising news about the family connection.

When they learned they were related, Christina and Makayla grew closer. They talked and texted about the regular teenage stuff, like school and boys. But they also confided about things you don't share with just anyone, like the hardships endured from the rampant alcoholism and drug addiction in their families. For Makayla, the family troubles and constant worry had left her with a deep insecurity.

"She was overly self-critical," said Christina. "Makayla was so beautiful, so smart, and so caring. But she didn't seem to see that. She thought she was inferior. And she sometimes let people walk all over her."

In a kind of unspoken pact, the girls looked out for each other.

"I was there for her," Christina said. "And she was there for me."

Since the seventh grade, Makayla had been living with her mom's brother, Patrick Dembkowski. Uncle Patrick—a union electrician with a beard, an earring, and tattoos on his forearms—led the life of a gentle, compassionate, and sober man.

He knew intimately the kind of trauma that Makayla had endured. His own mother—Makayla's grandmother—had been a drug addict. When Patrick was twelve, authorities took him and his siblings away from their mom.

"For a while, we bounced around from home to home," said Patrick, before the authorities ultimately placed the children with their father.

When Patrick was twenty, his mother died from an overdose of cocaine and oxycontin. All three of his mother's siblings were also addicts. Two were now dead. One had been in and out of drug treatment. Another had been jailed for his eighth DUI.

"I don't want you to end up like a lot of the family—on drugs or in jail," Patrick told her. "I worried sometimes that I was putting too much pressure on her, that she felt like she had to succeed or she'd be letting me down."

Uncle Patrick arranged for her to see a counselor. However heavy the depression may have weighed on Makayla, she always excelled at her studies. She worked hard at her job at a pet shop. And she showered attention on her two cats, Tiger and Luna, the latter a rescue she found abandoned in the driving rain at the beach.

Besides being a whiz with the school books, Makayla had a flair for drawing. She had an imagination for design that seemed almost magical. She aspired to become an architect.

Makayla mostly stayed home, often spending hours alone in her bedroom. She liked to play *The Sims*, a video simulation game in which the player creates virtual people, places them in houses, helps direct their moods, and satisfies their desires.

She didn't spend a lot of time in social cliques. Most students regarded her as something of a loner.

But during her sophomore year, something sparked her passion. It was a Give Back project, led by Christina, to distribute duffel bags to young foster children who had been abused. The student volunteers would raise funds to buy teddy bears, little blankets, crayons, and books, which they stuffed into the duffel bags for the kids. She logged more hours on the project than anyone else besides Christina.

"She had gone through struggles and she wanted to help others who struggled," said Christina. "Makayla helped others before she would help herself."

Makayla's mentor at Give Back, a twenty-two-year-old named Eliana Lozano, saw her fierce loyalty for the foster kids.

One afternoon, after Eliana drove over to pick her up for a mentoring session, Makayla jumped in the car and then suddenly shrieked with panic.

"The crayons! I'm missing the crayons!" she said, as she held her haul of other treats for the kids' duffel bags.

No worries, Eliana reassured her. They could stop at a cheap store and get what was needed.

But Makayla insisted that they go instead to Five Below, a trendier discount store. She didn't want the foster kids to have the kind of crayons that "crumble in your hands," as Makayla put it. To Eliana, the meaning was clear: Foster kids had gotten shortchanged in so many ways. At the very least, they deserved good crayons.

These seemed to be good times for Makayla. In a week or so, she and her mentor would be visiting the University of Delaware. "I've never been to the campus," Makayla had told the mentor with great anticipation. "And I'm going to be there for four years!"

The campus visit would never come. On a Friday evening toward the end of the school year, Makayla sent a text to Christina:

Heyy how are you?

Christina replied: *Good. What about you?*

Hours passed before a reply arrived.

Good, sorry forgot to send it, Makayla texted. *Summer break cannot come sooner.*

Something in the exchange caused Christina to worry about Makayla.

Yup, Christina texted back. *Are you ok?*

There would be no reply.

On that Friday night, Makayla was staying at her grandfather's house. As the hour grew late, she was surfing on her smartphone. She connected with someone on an anonymous chat room.

She agreed to meet a stranger at a nearby Dunkin' Donuts, and then sneaked out of her grandfather's place. Makayla and the stranger, a man from New Jersey, were later spotted on a security camera on the ninth floor of the parking garage at the Wilmington Hospital.

According to newspaper accounts, the man told police that he and Makayla had gone to the top of the parking garage for sex, but that she became distraught and started crying, so they stopped the physical encounter. Makayla was sixteen. The man was thirty-five.

It will never be known whether Makayla was panicked or overwhelmed with guilt. But a security camera recording clearly shows her final steps to the ledge of the nine-story building.

The gruesome headline blared: *Teen Jumps to Her Death from Wilmington Parking Garage*

The man reportedly told police that Makayla had claimed to be twenty-two.

The state's attorney told Uncle Patrick, who was consumed with grief, that he "really should talk to somebody."

Patrick replied that the only person he wanted to talk to was Makayla.

"I was devastated and I still am," said her Give Back mentor, Eliana. "I feel guilty. Maybe if I had pushed a little more to get her to open up and talk about things."

Christina fell into such deep denial—refusing at first to believe that the horrible news could be true—that she continued to send texts to Makayla, even as she realized the messages were futile.

I know you won't see this, but I love you, she texted.
I saw signs of you struggling and I tried to help. I didn't know you were so close. I didn't know that you were in trouble. I thought you were just going through a rough patch. I wish you were still here.
I miss you.

When Christina read the news account of Makayla's suicide, she grew angry. In the tawdry narrative of her death, nothing was said about Makayla's life—her loyalty and kindness, her stellar grades, her willingness to help abused children in need.

"She was such a good kid," said Christina. "And the article didn't say anything about that."

Makayla was buried at All Saints Cemetery in Wilmington. The week after her death, Makayla's report card arrived in the mail. Uncle Patrick gazed at the marks—straight As—and broke into wrenching sobs at what might have been, what should have been, for a girl with the potential of Makayla.

In Makayla's honor, Christina made plans to organize a club called Safe Space, a discussion group for students to talk about their feelings and troubles without fear of being judged or shunned.

"Mental health problems are not something we talk about," she said. "It's something we're ashamed about."

To fight the stigma, she posted messages targeted at students who might feel alone:

Speak up! Reach out! Suicide is preventable!

Christina, who planned to attend the University of Delaware on her Give Back scholarship, with plans of going on to medical school, said she hoped to channel her grief into accomplishment.

"Makayla can't live her life," she said. "I'm going to live my life in the way Makayla wanted to."

CHAPTER THIRTEEN

THE HOMECOMING

Feeling trapped, Mercedes had resigned herself to joining the military. Deep down, it wasn't what she really wanted. But it would be a way out of Millville, an escape from the town gossip and the whispering judgment about her family.

She wouldn't say so out loud, but it would also be a relief to step away from the heartache of her mother's addiction battle and the revolving jail stints, as well as her grandmother's severe bipolar swings, which lately had careened toward intense anger.

But going to college would not be a magic bullet, Mercedes decided. It would not liberate her from the trauma at home. She would still need to go back for holidays and breaks—and whenever else some emergency erupted that required this child to intervene as an adult.

There was another factor, too. Mercedes had serious doubts about whether she would be admitted to a college.

She had fallen behind when she dropped out of school during the last part of her junior year. Though she had returned to school in the fall, she had missed plenty of time in her senior year, too, much of it triggered by anxiety over the chaos at home. Deep into her final semester, the authorities at Millville High School had warned her: if you do not attend classes regularly through the rest of the semester, you will not be allowed to graduate.

Joining the military, besides erasing her worries about making the grade academically, offered one other bonus. She expected to be married and living on base with the young man who had been her boyfriend.

A couple of years older than Mercedes, he had been living with her in her grandmother's apartment. But it was a toxic relationship. He would put her down verbally and sometimes scared her.

She convinced herself that things between them would be better at a military base. She had been told that people in the armed services tended to marry early, and she counted on the bond of marriage to bring some peace and security to their relationship and her life.

And then she learned her boyfriend had another girlfriend.

She confronted him, pleading with him to tell her how they could fix things. He told her he was through with her. The next day, he moved his belongings out of the apartment.

Mom Maw was furious with Mercedes for somehow driving the boy away. The grandmother had been led to believe that he was contributing money toward the rent, and she fumed that now this source of income was gone.

In truth, the boyfriend had never contributed a penny. Mercedes had told her grandmother he was helping financially—a lie—so that she would be more amenable to allowing him to live in the apartment. Not only did he not ante up for rent, it was Mercedes who was giving *him* money—helping pay for his phone and his car insurance, among other things.

For all the problems, and the betrayal, she did not think she could live without him. Begging him to return, she repeatedly called and texted the boy. He never replied.

It triggered an even deeper downward spiral for Mercedes. When she went to school, she would sit in class and cry. Too depressed to eat, she lost more than twenty pounds. She began to cut herself, a ritual of self-harm that she had ended in the seventh grade. And then she took another dangerous and desperate step.

"I don't want to feel the way I am feeling any longer," she said.

She took a mouthful of her grandmother's sleeping pills. She wound up seeing a counselor at a medical center. After a long talk about her home life, she assured the counselor that she was not suicidal.

He gave her some advice: "I think you need a break from your family."

Mercedes trudged forward, but grew more and more isolated. People at Give Back, who had been urging her to apply for a college scholarship, were unable to reach her. Appointments were missed. Calls and texts went unanswered.

She would go to school, but spent most of the time sitting quietly in the guidance office. With only a few exceptions, she withdrew from her friends.

One of the exceptions was a boy named Maurice Lewis. She had worked with Maurice at McDonald's and they had developed a platonic friendship. Her old boyfriend, before the breakup, once left Mercedes stranded after the late shift. The boyfriend was angry that she wouldn't steal an order of Chicken McNuggets for him, so he sped off.

Maurice came to the rescue, giving Mercedes a ride home and a supportive talk: stay strong and follow the right path.

"He was a guy I could just be friends with," she explained, "and not have it be anything more than that."

Maurice was a well-behaved young man who did not use drugs or cause trouble. When she needed a friend, he was there.

Not long afterward, on a warm spring evening, Maurice was murdered.

To Mercedes, a world that seemed to make little sense now made no sense at all.

On a hot and humid Thursday morning in June, Mercedes struggled to get ready for the Millville High School graduation ceremony.

Her cap wouldn't fit over her curly hair and kept falling off. Her makeup dripped onto her gown. On what should have been one of the happiest days of her life, Mercedes burst into tears.

At the ceremony on the high school football field, Mercedes sat along with the others in folding chairs on the field and made small talk with classmates, most of them talking excitedly about their future plans.

"I'm going to the United States Air Force," Mercedes told anyone who asked, trying to keep up a cheerful and confident front.

"I put on this facade, but I didn't believe in myself," she later confided. "I hadn't taken any of the steps I needed to get into the military. I was stuck."

When her name was called, Mercedes walked across the stage to receive her diploma. The class president stepped toward her and gave her a hug, a tender gesture that suggested he knew the hard journey she had taken.

After the ceremony, the graduates sought out their families for the ritual of hugging and picture-taking. Mercedes found her family, among them her grandmother, an aunt, and her little brother, Marcus, who had tears in his eyes. He had posted on Instagram how proud he was of his big sister: *The first in the family to graduate!*

And there stood her mom. She had been released from jail just days earlier. She was very high. But as her grandmother pointed out, Mercedes should feel grateful that her mother had made it to the ceremony at all.

"My mom was a hot mess," Mercedes said. "She was so skinny. She was nodding off and making a clicking sound. And she hadn't showered."

Her father, as usual, was a no-show.

Other graduates and their families marched off to a celebratory dinner at a restaurant or a party at their houses. Mercedes's family didn't feel up for a celebration, so they just went home.

Mercedes attended an open house at the home of a football player. The celebration of the day temporarily lifted her spirits. But it wouldn't last.

In the following days, she felt like she was in a fog and carried heavy weights on her arms and legs.

She had pretty much given up on college and she had not followed through on any of the steps required to join the military.

As always, she did have a job. She spent most of her time at Dunkin' Donuts—working seven to twelve hours a day, six and sometimes seven days a week.

After work one day, she bumped into a cousin. The two of them sat for a talk. It seemed obvious that Mercedes wasn't in a good place. She gazed into the distance and when she spoke at all, she talked very, very slowly, as if it were difficult to get the words out.

"You are so depressed, Mercedes," the cousin told her. "You need help."

Melissa and others at Give Back had been worried about Mercedes. No one knew her whereabouts, her plans, or her state of mind. Melissa was determined to find her and provide some support. The fact that Melissa herself had just gotten out of the hospital, and was recovering from meningitis, was not going to stop her.

Using her computer to search for clues, Melissa found that she and Mercedes shared fifteen Facebook friends, most of them connected to the First Star organization for foster kids.

She blasted a group message to the shared friends: *How do you know Mercedes Marquez?*

Julio Nieves, a First Star program director who volunteered at the Delanco church camp, responded almost immediately.

She's a camp kid, he texted.

This was eerie. Delanco was a camp that had been founded by Melissa's family a century ago.

Melissa explained to Julio that Mercedes had not been responding to messages: "She's gone dark on us."

Julio promised: "I'll text her right now."

The message beeped for Mercedes just after being told by her cousin that she needed help.

Hey Mercedes, where you been? Julio asked. *I need to connect with you.*

Mercedes had attended the church camp for about a decade, starting at age six, but she had been absent for the past few years.

I'm not doing good, Mercedes replied. *I've been going through it. Just trying to get it together really.*

Will you let me help? Julio asked her. *I know things are hard.*

He added: *One of my people is Melissa Helmbrecht.*

Mercedes searched her memory.

"Wow! That name is familiar," she thought.

And then it dawned on her that Melissa was one of the people she had met with the Give Back scholarship program.

Melissa called me asking about you, Julio told her. *Would you come visit camp with her?*

Really? Mercedes asked. *How?*

I mean it, Julio assured her. *I have a team that wants to care for you. A lot more than you can imagine.*

He added: *Heck, if you want to come out tonight, you're in. Just let me know.*

Mercedes explained that she didn't have a way to get to the camp. She didn't have a suitcase of clothes for the week-long camp. And she couldn't afford to miss work.

During the back-and-forth of the texting, meanwhile, Julio and Melissa had been talking on the phone. Melissa assured him that Mercedes would have everything she needed—a ride to camp, a suitcase of clothes, money for her lost wages.

Julio texted Mercedes that everything had been arranged.

We got you, he told Mercedes. *This might just be a gift from above.*

I'm speechless, she texted. *Honestly?*

I'll send the limo, he told her, referring to Melissa's minivan.

He told her to be ready in an hour.

Mercedes ran home and scrambled to pull together a few things for her stay at the camp. Melissa called, asking for her address.

"I'll pack you a suitcase," Melissa told her. "Whatever you need—body wash, clothes. We can go to Walmart and get it all."

About forty-five minutes later, Melissa, wearing her First Star shirt, pulled up to Mercedes's apartment house in her minivan.

Mercedes felt more hopeful than she had in a very long time, but at the same time, she was more than a little nervous.

"I was worried that I'd have to explain myself," Mercedes said later. "But all Melissa cared about was, 'Are you okay?'"

On the drive to the church camp, located in aptly named Tabernacle, New Jersey, Mercedes felt comfortable enough with Melissa to let down her guard. In tears, she told her everything: the latest troubles at home, the abuse and betrayal by the boyfriend, the murdered friend, her overwhelming feelings of anxiety and doubt. Mercedes cried long and hard.

"You're safe now," Melissa told her. "Whether you join the military or not, I want you to have a game plan. We're going to work on this."

Stepping out of the minivan, Mercedes walked tentatively onto the grounds of the camp. She wondered and worried about what people were going to think.

"Hey, girl, we missed you here!" shouted Tim, a youth pastor, whose eyes welled up when he saw Mercedes. "Where have you been?"

"Lost," she responded.

Being at the camp was a homecoming.

"The kids were so happy to see me," she said. "Just being around all that love—I was back. It was the resurrection of Mercedes."

At the camp, there was camaraderie, joking around, hugging, reflection, crazy games—one contest involved trying to grab hold of a greased watermelon—and some prayer.

"That's something I hadn't done in a really long time," she said.

Toward the end of the week, Mercedes started feeling anxiety and a sense of dread that camp was coming to an end. She would be returning to her troubles.

Whenever anyone asked, she remained adamant that her plan was fixed: she was joining the military.

Julio saw through her. Although he was a generation older than Mercedes, he was also a product of the struggles of Cumberland County. He sat her down and looked her in the eye. He said he worried that she was joining the military, not because she had a special passion for the armed services—an honorable path for many—but because she wanted to run away. That wasn't a good reason to choose a career.

"Well, I don't want to go home," she told Julio.

"You don't have to," he told her.

"How's that?" she asked.

He told her that Melissa and her husband wanted her to make a home with their family.

Mercedes was skeptical.

When she arrived to pick up Mercedes, Melissa asked her directly: "Will you come home and live with me? You don't have to commit to forever. We can take it one day at a time."

Julio, who stood six feet, five inches, towered nearby.

"Mercedes wants to know," he told Melissa, "'What's the catch?'"

"There is none," Melissa replied. "We just want to love you."

Mercedes would later describe it as "the easiest and hardest decision I've ever had to make."

For Melissa, it was simple.

"I didn't think she'd be alive in a year otherwise."

When the minivan pulled up to Melissa's family home, Mercedes looked around and felt a culture shock.

"I lived in this little apartment in a rough neighborhood in a poor town," she said. "And I see this nice house. And there's grass! And nearby there are cornfields!"

The church camp offered Melissa a job working at the camp the following week–an offer she instantly accepted– so she would be returning to Tabernacle in just a day or so.

Without much time to spare, Melissa and Mercedes hurried off to Walmart for clothes and other essentials. She was told she could buy anything she wanted–an invitation for most kids to splurge. But she did not take advantage.

"She bought three basic items," said Melissa, "and said, 'That's all I need.'"

Mercedes had still not addressed her future, but Melissa wanted her to count on one thing.

"Whether you join the military or not, when you come home, you're coming to our house," she told her. "From here on out, you're safe."

Mercedes was quiet for a moment.

"I trusted how genuine Melissa was," Mercedes said. "She had so much faith in me that I started to have faith in myself."

CHAPTER FOURTEEN

WHO I AM

Kimberly Ledwell was wearing the pale blue uniform reserved for a disgraced woman who lived in a cage. Along with dozens of other inmates, she was escorted one morning from her cell through noisy, sometimes dangerous hallways, to a concrete block gymnasium—as cold as stone—situated deep in the bowels of a rural Illinois prison that was too far to locate for anyone, unless they were desperately lost.

Almost thirty-four, Kim took her seat on a metal folding chair alongside the other women, as guards monitored their steps. The inmates were uncertain about the purpose of the meeting. Most of them, including Kim, had been told only that the conference had something to do with their children. Many of these were mothers who had scant contact with their kids, often not spending even a single second in a year with them, or two years, or more.

Many of them had been written off by their kids. Some women knew that their children hated them. But if there was some way they could stand up for their kids, they would stand up, shackled or not.

In this environment, it was startling to see a civilian. The prisoners spotted a petite woman in jeans who stood beneath a basketball hoop. The woman from the outside was Melissa, of Give Back. She was prepared to talk to the women in a way that recognized that they were more than simply a number and a record of mistakes.

Melissa had come from her Give Back office in New Jersey to the Logan Correctional Center for women to talk about painful troubles, including her own.

For a woman who seemed to have everything that these prisoners craved, especially freedom, Melissa's first words were startling.

"I was a high school dropout," she acknowledged. "I had a lot of struggles. I was the worst student in my class. But I was fortunate to meet a mentor who transformed my life."

Melissa talked about her journey as a lost teenager, growing up in a troubled household. She told these prisoners, women who were not accustomed to getting a break, that Give Back was making a special outreach to students with incarcerated parents, especially those with mothers who had gone to jail. The women seemed to sit taller in their seats, listening intently to her words.

How many of the women, Melissa asked, had children who were still in school?

Almost every hand in the gymnasium was raised.

Melissa asked how many of them wanted their children to attend college.

Nearly every hand reached skyward.

"We want to help your children go to college," Melissa told them, "and to graduate with a degree."

For some of the women, it was a rare occasion to be recognized as loving mothers, rather than bad examples.

One woman, speaking in a quavering voice, lamented that she wasn't sure about her kids' classroom performance, explaining, "I don't get to communicate with my children as much as I'd like."

Melissa responded in a way that gave the woman reason to hope. The inmates were given forms to grant permission, if they wished, to Give Back staff to contact the legal guardians of the children, as well as the students themselves, and inform them about the scholarship program and its requirements. After Melissa spoke, a long line of women stepped from their chairs and walked to drop off the forms.

Most of the women were soft-spoken, often a bit shy, usually embarrassed, as they handed over the permission papers and then made their way back to their narrow cells.

But when Kim Ledwell stepped toward Melissa, she stopped in her tracks, stood firm, and spoke with a tone of insistence.

"She was adamant," said Melissa. "She implored me: 'My kid's the one for this scholarship program.'"

Kim's daughter, Skye, was a freshman at a Joliet high school in Will County in Illinois, not far from where I grew up. She described her daughter as a top-notch student, a girl with outstanding character, and a kid who could really use a break.

As Melissa put it, "This wasn't a mom I expected to see in jail. This was a PTA mom."

Skye, a high school freshman, was living with her grandfather, a disabled construction worker who had quit drinking many years ago.

Melissa called Skye and her grandpa and explained that Give Back offered the chance for a full-ride scholarship to college. Each of them fairly gasped.

"I think they thought we were crazy," said Melissa.

Melissa called the Give Back office in Lockport, Illinois, and alerted Steve Cardamone, who heads the group in the state, to keep an eye open for an application from Skye. When he received a report about Skye from her high school guidance counselor, Cardamone remembered thinking: "This is a kid we've got to have."

Skye was a student who took tough classes and earned top grades. Told about the Give Back requirement to maintain a 3.0 grade point average, she responded with the shrugging confidence of a kid who had proven her academic mettle.

"That's too easy," she said. "I'll keep my GPA above 3.5."

Skye was a midfielder on the school soccer team. She participated as a cheerleader, both on the squad that led the crowds at the football and basketball games, but also on the elite, competitive cheer squad that competed in playoffs and made it to the Illinois state tournament. A straight arrow, she attended church on Sunday and Wednesday nights. And she met regularly with Pastor Seth for guidance to stay on the right path.

As with all of the applicants, Skye was required to complete an essay and sit for an interview. She mentioned her mom's circumstances in the essay. But she never brought it up in the interview, even though the Give Back staff tried mightily to engage her about her hardships.

"These are kids who have stories that will break your heart, but they'll never bring it up in conversation," Steve explained. "They pretty much take the attitude: 'That's not me. I'm going to tell you *who I am.*'"

When Skye ultimately received the verdict from Give Back, she talked on the phone to her mom in prison, who was nervously waiting for news about the scholarship application.

"I got a letter in the mail," Skye told her mom, slowly drawing out the news, trying to heighten the drama.

"It starts out this way," her daughter told her.

Congratulations!

Her mother could scarcely contain herself. "I wanted to tell everybody," she said. "The women in prison had already seen pictures of her, so they felt like they knew her. When I told the other women about the scholarship, I said: 'See, it can be done!'"

Her daughter's triumph brought Kim back to memories of herself as a kid, when everything seemed possible and she was primed to conquer the world. In those early days, she had known a taste of glory like few other teenagers. As a freshman and sophomore in high school, she had qualified for the National Junior Olympics and competed in the pole vault and relay races.

But with so much trouble at home—her parents' alcohol problems and her mom's mental illness, her parents splitting up, lots of moving around—Kim lost her way.

While still a child herself, Kim gave birth to her first child. She named her Autumn. When the baby was only twenty-nine days old, Kim brought her into bed late one night. While they were sleeping, the new mother rolled over on the baby and suffocated her.

After the tragedy, Kim escaped into alcohol, cocaine, and other drugs.

"The guilt was so overwhelming," she said. "I didn't want to feel anything."

She became pregnant again, once more in an unstable relationship, and she ran as far away as a poor, frightened girl could go. Homeless for much of the time, she ultimately gave birth to Skye—named because "the sky was the limit for her." Not much more than a year later, she had another baby, a boy she named Devan.

She stayed clean for three years. But then she was involved in a car accident that left her seriously injured. The doctor prescribed painkillers. She was soon hooked on drugs again.

In Florida, Kim's life spiraled even further out of control. She ended up in jail for a stretch. Her son lived with Kim's friend, a woman who had been a police officer. Skye was shipped to Illinois to live with her grandparents.

It would not be the last of Kim's troubles. Charged and convicted of battery, robbery, and manufacture of methamphetamine, she was sentenced to three years.

Hours before her mother died, Kim called from prison. Her mother could not speak, but a nurse put the phone to her ear.

"I'm sorry," Kim told her mother, who was unable to respond. "It was the drugs. I didn't want things to be this way. Know that I love you."

On the day Kim was released from prison, she was given an Amtrak train ticket to Chicago and a ten-dollar bill. She carried all of her belongings in a small box. When the train made a stop in Joliet, about an hour south of Chicago, Kim got off.

In a driving blizzard, Kim looked up to see her father's car pull up to the station. She saw a car door swing open. There was Skye, all arms and legs, racing excitedly toward her mother. The two of them locked in a long, tight embrace.

That night, Kim crawled into bed with Skye at the grandpa's house. The mom and daughter talked late into the night.

At her own choosing, Kim checked herself into a sober-living home in Joliet. She vowed to spend several months at the house, determined to get healthy, work enough to build some savings, become emotionally and financially grounded enough to rent a home, and have Skye and Devan move in with her.

"I know this chance is one in a lifetime," said Kim, "and it will never come again."

She worked sixty hours a week and more. Her main job was moving packages in a warehouse, working an eleven-hour shift, lifting heavy packages to shelves above her head. She also worked for a landscaper – "I cut grass, move dirt, plant flowers" – and worked a third job at a loan office.

At the sober house, where each woman was required to hold a job, Kim was the building maintenance officer. She fastened toilet seats, repaired the lawnmower, and fixed pretty much anything that was broken.

Kim was allowed to leave two nights a week for sleepovers, and she would spend those nights with Skye. On other nights, Skye came to stay at the sober house. Devan came up from Florida to stay with her, too. Every day, and sometimes twice a day, Kim attended a meeting of Alcoholics Anonymous.

"I sometimes take Skye to meetings with me," she said. "I want her to know what I'm doing to make a better life for us."

Kim had lately taken to drawing. In her craft, she had come to realize that the most important part of creating a piece of art was not just the drawing itself, but knowing what to erase. It was a lot like life.

Learning to live outside prison had been difficult, but Kim was learning to adjust.

"At first, I was skittish, like a cat wanting to run under the table," she said. "At AA meetings, I'd get so nervous about speaking that I'd have to run to the bathroom and throw up."

She cultivated a community to lean on. On her Facebook account, she had at least one hundred friends in recovery, some of them still behind bars.

As mom and daughter, Kim and Skye were "sort of growing up together," as each of them put it. They would hang out at Dunkin' Donuts whenever they could, talk about the day and sip caramelized ice coffee, or feast on cheese fries at Mr. Submarine's.

In the evenings, they spent most of their time watching movies and television shows. Skye was obsessed with *Grey's Anatomy*. "I've watched each episode at least five times," she said.

Skye liked the show because she had watched her mom and her grandmother hospitalized for illnesses, and wanted to become a caretaker herself someday.

For her sophomore year, she signed up for classes that put her on a path to choose almost any career: Honors Advanced Algebra, Honors English II, Physics, Spanish II, and Medical Biology.

For all of her successes, Skye had come to terms that some heartbreak cannot be healed. Earlier in the summer, her mom had saved for a special trip. She took Skye to Florida see her father, a man the girl had never met.

They planned to spend a week together. She hoped that she and her dad would learn about what they had in common. They would take walks along the beach. They would try to establish bonds for the first time.

But when Skye and her mom arrived in Florida, the dad sent a text saying he was too busy to see his daughter, even for a moment.

Skye tried to take it in stride. Her father had sent her one hundred dollars, so she went to the mall and made the best of it. There was too much excitement ahead, as she zoomed through high school, to let herself feel down.

The idea of performing as a cheerleader in the packed football stadium and the roar-filled basketball gymnasium, and riding a float in the homecoming parade – "we get to throw out candy to the little kids" – brought a smile to the teenager's face.

And then there was soccer. That was a big deal in a sports-crazed town like Joliet.

Skye was a star midfielder on the team. But she feared losing her spot. She had suffered an injury before her sophomore season. The doctor fitted her with a boot, gave her some crutches, and told her she would have to take it easy and skip tryouts.

But Skye was a girl accustomed to overcoming adversity. She had survived far worse than a painful foot.

When the time came for tryouts, she left behind the boot and crutches. She gritted her teeth and jogged to the soccer tryout.

Skye was a survivor. More than that, she was a winner.

"If I can walk, I can run," she told herself. "And if I can run, I can play."

She took to the soccer field and dazzled everyone who watched her. Despite the pain, she easily made the team.

Her triumph against the odds seemed destined to be the story of her life.

CHAPTER FIFTEEN

LAUNDRY BASKET AS LUGGAGE

Riccardo Dale was a refugee. He was not from a faraway, war-torn land. He was a teenager from New Jersey. But he was fleeing a dangerous place, and he had nowhere to go. He owned a small laundry basket, which held all of his earthly belongings.

Just out of high school, he hadn't applied to college. Working long hours at a warehouse and riding his bicycle to work, he had been surviving as a couch surfer—sleeping on living room sofas or in the basements of people who offered him temporary shelter—a respite from dangerous neighborhoods and a troubled home life. But his options had run out.

When Melissa learned about the homeless young man, she organized a rescue.

"We'll pick you up in an hour," she told Riccardo. "Be ready."

Melissa was working that summer with the First Star
college immersion program for high school foster kids at
Rowan University in New Jersey.

Struck by Riccardo's smarts, survival skills, and compassion
for others, First Star hired him as a mentor for the younger foster
kids in the program. It didn't pay much, but the gig would allow
him to live in a dormitory for the summer. That would solve his
housing plight, at least temporarily.

Riccardo had been alone in the world, for all practical
purposes, since he ran away as a sophomore in high school.
His mother, who was addicted to drugs and alcohol and
suffered with mental illness, lived in a world of instability and
desperation. At least once, she had tried to kill herself in front
of her son.

Riccardo's father, for his part, had long ago abandoned
the family. He moved to Jamaica and never once looked back.
At least that was how Riccardo saw it.

From the time he was a toddler, Riccardo was moved around
from place to place, a vagabond from the start. These were
neighborhoods often terrorized by the gunfire of street gangs.

But it was even more dangerous at home. As a boy of five
or six, Riccardo's babysitter would call him vicious names and
smack him with pots and pans. And then came the punishment
that would mark him for life.

The babysitter pushed him down in a tub of scalding water and held him there, as he screamed in pain for what seemed like an eternity. In a horrifying torture he would never forget, skin melted away from parts of his body. In excruciating pain and badly injured from the torment, Riccardo was hospitalized. With the help of doctors and physical therapists, he learned to walk again.

He had been burned so deeply that the scars never quite healed. As if that weren't difficult enough, he endured bullying from other kids for his injuries. When he would go to a swimming pool or a locker room, the kids would sometimes tease him.

"Hey, *burnt feet!*" he remembered some of them laughingly call out in ridicule.

Even during the most difficult of those times, Riccardo drew a measure of strength and comfort from his stepfather. He was a man who had served time in prison for at least two stretches. Whatever his wrongdoing, his stepfather had shown attention, love, and a tenderness that Riccardo had not otherwise known.

"He wasn't perfect," as Riccardo put it, "but he was the only male figure in my life who cared about me."

During Riccardo's freshman year of high school, the stepfather died in jail, sending Riccardo into a downward emotional spiral. For a boy starved for any glimmer of approval, it was a devastating loss.

At age fifteen, Riccardo was working two jobs. At the end of his sophomore year, he decided to run away. He chose an unlikely destination—a prestigious prep school. He showed up unannounced at Doane Academy, a highly respected private school in Burlington, New Jersey, a rigorous, buttoned-down institution founded in 1837. The yearly tuition was nearly $20,000.

Riccardo was honest with the admissions officials: he had neither the money nor the grades to qualify for Doane.

But he begged to be accepted.

Impressed by Riccardo's courage and determination, along with a certain uncommon intelligence that distinguished him from bright, but sheltered suburban kids, the school agreed to take him as a scholarship student. In this rigorous academic environment, Doane Academy told him he would need to repeat his sophomore year, a mandate that Riccardo was smart enough to know he needed.

He moved in with the family of a boy who was enrolled at Doane and had been a teammate with Riccardo on a club basketball team. Despite his scars, and a bit of an awkward gait while moving on the court, Riccardo could still play the game.

When Riccardo was a senior, I was asked to speak at the graduation for Doane. While I was there, the headmaster, George Sanderson, introduced me to the young man, along with a handful of other disadvantaged students. I quickly learned that Riccardo was special.

Riccardo and some of the other students were given a copy of my memoir, *Through the Fires*, which touched on my own family problems as a kid. Riccardo read the book and took it to heart. On the day that he was rescued by Melissa, with his belongings in the laundry basket, the book sat on top.

The dean of students at Rowan University, Richard Jones, learned about Riccardo and his remarkable skills as a mentor for foster kids in the summer immersion program. The dean was so impressed that he offered Riccardo admission to the school. He arranged for Riccardo to live year-round in a dormitory, so he would never have to worry about where he was going to go during holidays and other school breaks. Give Something Back awarded him a scholarship.

Riccardo stands out on the Rowan campus. He makes it a point to dress sharply, often wearing a tie or turtleneck to class.

"It's not easy, but I put a smile on my face and act like everything's cool," he said. "I'm not going to dress or carry myself in a way that lets you think I'm nothing, that I'm from the streets, that I'm 'hood.'"

At first, some other students at Rowan made the mistake of assuming that Riccardo came from a pampered and privileged background.

They would soon learn otherwise.

Riccardo became a natural leader on campus. He started a mentoring group called Free All Minds that specialized in working with young black men and boys who had known adversity.

He recruited other mentors – black males who shared a challenging background – and they accompanied him to elementary and high schools to counsel and inspire disadvantaged students.

"For kids who have experienced abuse or foster care, I can relate," Riccardo explained. "If a mentor comes from a comfortable life with a white picket fence, the disadvantaged kids will tend to think to themselves, 'Yeah, but you don't *really* know.'"

"With me, it's different," Riccardo said. "*I really do know.*"

When talking to young people who had been dealt a tough hand, he would let down his guard and commiserate.

"At the end of the day, you want to hear your parents tell you they're proud of you – and when you don't hear 'I love you,' it's tough."

He would tell them about how he ultimately decided to take control of his life.

"When kids tell me about their tough circumstances, I'll say, 'Yeah, that's really messed up.' But if you're waiting for somebody to save you, they're not coming. I finally realized it wasn't going to do any good for me to say, 'Mom, stop being an addict!' or 'Dad, come back and be proud of me!'"

That was simply not going to happen. And all the wishing or complaining was not going to change a thing.

"My mom was not going to give me a hug," he would explain. "And my dad wasn't going to come back and tell me he's proud of me."

But there was hope. As Riccardo would tell the kids, you didn't need to follow the path you'd been given. You could show the world you were meant for better things.

Riccardo became a mentor to a small army of kids who had known hurt and trouble. One of them was Will Denson, the foster kid who had been abused as a child and was among the First Star students to be promised a college scholarship by Give Back.

When Riccardo learned that Will had been wearing pretty much the same clothes for three years, and outgrowing them, he organized a clothing drive for him. He even gave Will twenty bucks–about all that Riccardo had to his name–so that he could get a better haircut.

"Riccardo is like a big brother to me," Will explained. "He taught me about the importance of my appearance. I was dressing like I didn't care who I was."

Under Riccardo's tutelage, Will's look changed. When he arrived at the college immersion summer program at Rowan, Will looked like he had just stepped out of the pages of a *GQ* magazine: crisp black T-shirt, tan slacks cuffed at the ankle, argyle socks, and two-tone dress shoes. The new look, of course, wasn't the only thing inspired by Riccardo. So was Will's attitude.

The high school years for Will had not been easy. In Riccardo, he found someone who could relate to his circumstances – and give him a push to lift himself up.

Riccardo even helped Will, an aspiring musician, produce and record his first song. It was called "Battle Cry."

The song addressed Will's mother's addiction, but pledged that he would remain loving and loyal to her forever.

Is that the reason you drink? a lyric called out. *No matter what, I'll always be here for you. You'll always be my mom.*

Not long after he recorded the song, his mother entered a treatment program. On the day of Will's graduation from Delsea Regional High School, a day he acknowledged he "wasn't always sure would ever come," his mom sat beaming in the audience, clean and sober and proud.

She was so proud that she wept. And her son was so proud of her – and himself – that he had to fight back tears.

There wasn't money for a big commencement open house party for Will, the sort of bash that a lot of high school graduates take for granted. But the celebration would be no less gratifying.

After the ceremony, Will, his mom, and his two brothers went back to her little apartment. There was an abundance of fried chicken, mashed potatoes, mac and cheese – and a shared sense of joy and accomplishment that an important corner in life had been turned, for both mother and son.

"We talked and laughed so much," said Will, breaking into a smile at the thought of it.

He was set to enter Rowan College at Gloucester County, the first in the family to make it to college. The transition was being eased by the college immersion program, where he took classes in English and math, as well as a course called Life Skills, which focused on techniques for controlling emotions. The students even learned yoga.

"Yoga," said Will, "is great for a sense of peace."

Riccardo, for his part, completed his sophomore year at Rowan University with solid grades, winning the affection and appreciation of many students and faculty members, including Dean Jones, who had taken a chance on the homeless young man.

"I was impressed with his perseverance, his resilience, his drive and dedication," the dean said.

Jones saw in Riccardo a kindred spirit. While the dean hadn't experienced quite as rough a life in his own childhood, he knew the feeling of coming home to a house darkened because the electricity had been shut off for nonpayment of the utility bill.

"I appreciate and recognize struggle," the dean said. "I was a rowdy kid. I had relatives who said I was going to end up in jail."

Students with a harsh upbringing, like Riccardo had experienced, are not rarities. Studies show the demand for mental health services on campuses nationwide has increased sharply in recent years, as students arrive at college emotionally shaken by traumas in childhood.

Between 2009 and 2015, the number of students visiting counseling centers increased some 30 percent, according to a study by the Center for Collegiate Mental Health.

The dean would see Riccardo on campus and check to make sure he was doing okay. The two became close enough that Riccardo came to regard him as an uncle, calling him "Unc." The dean, meanwhile, saw the young man as family. At Thanksgiving, the dean made a place for Riccardo at the dinner table.

Dean Jones discovered quickly that this was no ordinary college student. As a "meticulous dresser," as the dean put it, Riccardo was making a statement to the world that he was a serious young man with serious plans.

But it was more than the clothes. "He says 'hello,' he looks you in the eye, he remembers your name," said Dean Jones. "He has the ability to make everyone feel special."

Like many other schools, Rowan University reserved a spot on its Board of Trustees for a student elected by peers. At Rowan, the student trustee served as an advisor during the junior year, and then assumed voting power as a trustee in the senior year. It was a big deal. The student trustee had the same say on important college matters, such as tuition and admission policies, as anyone else on the board.

Toward the end of his sophomore year, Riccardo decided to run for a spot on this august board. Three other smart and ambitious Rowan students also ran for the coveted seat.

The winner, in a landslide, was Riccardo.

CHAPTER SIXTEEN

FINDING THE WAY

Mercedes had been telling everyone at church camp she was definitely joining the military.

But Melissa wanted Mercedes to have some options. With just weeks remaining before the fall term, she reached out to Rowan College to ask if there was any way possible, at this late date, that Mercedes could be admitted. After hearing her story, the president of the college, Fred Keating, vowed to move heaven and earth to make it happen, as long as Mercedes truly wanted to attend.

Melissa gave the heads-up to a CASA volunteer at the church camp. The volunteer told Mercedes that Rowan College would be willing to hold a seat for her. But did she really *want* to go to college?

Mercedes cried so hard her body shuddered.

"Yes!" she said, with what breath she could find. "This is really happening! I don't know how, but it's happening. I can do this!"

As soon as she left church camp for Melissa's house, Mercedes went to work on the necessary paperwork for admission to college. She was going to need to move fast. School would start in just a few weeks.

Every morning, she rose early and attacked her to-do list. She needed to secure vital documents, high school transcripts, tax statements, medical records. Most difficult of all, she needed to find a document that explained her custody status. That was going to be difficult since her grandmother, angry about Mercedes's decision to move out, had pretty much stopped speaking with her.

Mercedes sat down and wrote a letter to Judge Harold U. Johnson of the Family Division of Superior Court in Cumberland County.

> My name is Mercedes Marquez and I am writing this letter to you to explain my situation and why I am requesting my grandmother Debra Futrell's custody papers for me.
>
> My grandmother has had custody of me for as long as I can remember. As much as I appreciate everything she has done for me, these past few years my situation has been a tough one.
>
> I've been paying my grandmother's rent since I was fifteen years old and once our food stamps were cut in 2016, I've been supplying our food as well. It wasn't easy, but it was what I was asked to do and I couldn't let her down.
>
> My grandmother has major depressive disorder as well as many other mental health issues, making our living situation

a very cold one. She has been in and out of hospitals, mental health institutions, and even homes.

My mother has had a heroin addiction my entire life and has spent most of her life in and out of jails, making it very difficult to hold a relationship with her.

Due to my mother being incarcerated in the winter of 2016, the Give Back Foundation offered me a full ride scholarship to Rowan University. Around this time, my mother also became sober and I finally began to have a relationship with her… for the first time in my entire life I felt as if I finally had her.

In January of 2017, my mother relapsed and it hurt me in ways I couldn't explain. I couldn't understand why I wasn't able to fill her void the way that she had fulfilled mine and I became very depressed.

Depression is something that is very common in my family but when it came to dealing with mine, it was never an option. I had rent to pay, a family to feed, school to attend, and a scholarship to keep.

I felt as though I was carrying the weight of the world on my shoulders and became a very anxious person. I began to worry about my mother like never before. When she needed money, I was there. When she needed clothes, I was there. But it hurt when I realized she only called when she needed something and never just to call.

*I started having panic attacks in school and I no longer
wanted to go. In March of 2017 my grandmother signed
me out of high school. It seemed as though she had what she
needed for rent and for food, what I did didn't really matter."*

She told the judge that she later came to realize that quitting
high school wasn't a good idea. If she returned to school, she
had learned, she could stay with her class since she had built
up enough credits by doubling up on math classes and taking
advanced level courses.

*My grandmother wasn't too supportive of me going back
because now I worked less, which meant less money.
My senior year I still had to deal with everything I was
dealing with the previous year, but I knew if I put my
mind to it, I would be able to graduate.*

*I still paid my grandmother rent, but the closer I got to
turning eighteen, the more distant she grew from me.
Each argument came with accusations of leaving her and
before I knew it each argument came with a 'Get out
Mercedes.' I was no longer welcomed at my own house.*

*I endured everything as well as I could but then in May of
2018, one of my best friends was murdered… leading me
into my deepest depression yet.*

*I no longer kept in touch with the Give Back Foundation
and I felt stuck. I graduated high school but still felt I could
do no right. I felt as if I had no purpose. I thought paying rent
and supplying food and dealing with my mother's addiction*

and grandmother's depression was what life was about and I was no longer driven.

She told the judge that when she was contacted by Give Back, she shared her feelings about feeling "trapped" and "without a purpose."

> *Melissa offered me to move in with her to give me a solid foundation that I could build on. She taught me life was not supposed to be how it's been for me and gave me hope for my future…*
>
> *On August 8th of 2018, I was told the president of Rowan College would push me through…Due to my case being so special, as well as so late, Rowan University is pushing me to obtain any record I can explaining my situation.*
>
> *This would be difficult either way, but because I no longer live with my grandmother, she feels a sense of abandonment and isn't speaking to me much or willing to help me obtain any records I need.*
>
> *In the past week, I have obtained my high school transcript, a state ID, my official birth certificate and my Tax Return information.*
>
> *My custody paper is the last item on my list and I would forever be grateful if I could obtain this record so I am able to start at Rowan in the fall of 2018. Thank you for your time and consideration.*
>
> *Sincerely,*
>
> *Mercedes Marquez*

Mercedes would participate in the unusual Rowan Choice program. She would begin her studies at Rowan College, on the two-year associate's track, with a guarantee of acceptance to the bachelor's program at Rowan University if she performed adequately.

In the Choice program, the community college students lived in residential housing on the university campus and took part in the activities of the larger school. In essence, students were able to attend the two-year college while living on the campus of the four-year school, all the while building a crucial network of support for first-generation students and those who had overcome serious challenges.

She texted her mother and grandmother to keep them up to date with her college plans. She received no reply. She did manage to reach her grandmother on the telephone.

"I'm not abandoning you," Mercedes tried to explain to her. "But all I've got is a high school degree and a crappy job. I've got to plan for the future."

And that meant going to college. Mercedes asked if she could take Mom Maw to lunch before she left for school.

Her grandmother declined.

With her college paperwork completed, Mercedes traveled with Melissa to Rowan to take the placement exams that gauge a student's level of preparedness. Mercedes scored high enough to exempt her from any remedial courses, a highly unusual feat for a student in the First Star foster care group in South Jersey.

"She's brilliant," said Melissa. "If she had grown up in another environment, she would have been the valedictorian."

And when Melissa discovered Mercedes's aptitude with the computer, she hired her as her part-time coordinator of social media, a weekend job that came with a desk in the Bridgeton office as well as a modest salary.

"I've even got my own business card," said Mercedes. "That's pretty cool."

Melissa took Mercedes to our Princeton headquarters, where I got the chance to congratulate her in person, give her a hug, and tell her how proud she had made all of us.

It was clear that living with Melissa's family had been good for Mercedes.

"Even when she's gone for work," said Mercedes, "she texts to tell me that she loves me and that I'm going to change the world."

Mercedes had tagged along with the family on Back to School Night for little Wally. When it was time for introductions, Wally Sr. rose to point out his loved ones.

"That's my wife, Melissa, my son, Wally, my daughter Chloe," he said, and then after the slightest of pauses, he added, "And that's my other daughter, Mercedes."

Little Wally broke into a big smile and fairly shouted in excitement, "Is she ours now?"

"Yeah," said Wally Sr., "she is."

"I have these amazing people who love me," Mercedes would say later. "So I can't be that bad."

Mercedes felt a sense of peace, comfort and security that she had never experienced before. She was deeply grateful.

She knew that Melissa, a big fan of the Jamaican reggae artist, Bob Marley, had a birthday coming up. Mercedes planned to get Melissa a bracelet with three miniature bird charms. It would be a nod to Marley's famous anthem, "Three Little Birds," best known for its refrain, *Every little thing is gonna be all right.*

The words seemed to capture the positive vibes that Mercedes was feeling.

On the night before leaving for Rowan College, Mercedes was a bundle of nerves.

"It's a happy kind of nervous," she said. "I got like two hours of sleep because I was so excited. I just sat on my bed and thought, 'Wow, I'm going to college.'"

In the morning, she boarded Melissa's minivan with her clothes and toiletries. Her hair was tied in a bun and she toted a black backpack. Domenic had come for the trip, along with Julio, and even little Wally and Chloe.

Like the other foster care students, Mercedes had been given a Desk in a Box, a container that included a book bag, pencils, binder, scissors, staples, flash drive, sticky notes, index cards, and other academic tools of the trade. They were the essentials that most kids take for granted on shopping trips with their parents. She also brought a lava lamp, a gift from Melissa.

"It's the college experience," Melissa told her with a smile. "You've got to have a lava lamp."

The College Express minivan rolled down South Jersey country roads past barns, horses, cows, grain silos, and fields of tomatoes. As the old farmhouses grew distant in the rearview mirror, the minivan passed newer subdivisions and strip malls, and finally, took the exit for Glassboro, the home of Rowan.

Mercedes saw the campus in the distance, the august academic halls of wisdom, the beautiful greensward with towering oaks, the funky restaurants. And young people were everywhere—on foot, on bicycles, on skateboards.

As she took in the scene, her eyes lit up like Las Vegas.

"I'm super stoked," she said.

Mercedes and her posse decamped at the café in the fashionable Barnes & Noble bookstore on campus and examined the school's moving day instructions—a long list that included the location of the orientation and directions for signing up for the cafeteria meal plan.

And then they waded into the crowds of students and parents on a day that marked one of the biggest turning points of their lives.

At last, Mercedes found her residence hall, Holly Pointe, a gleaming yellow and white building in the heart of campus life. It all felt a little surreal. As she walked the hall in search of her room number, a part of her worried that something might still go wrong and she would be denied entrance to college.

Her hands trembled as she inserted the key into the lock and pushed open the door to her room. She stepped inside and fell silent for a bit as she glanced around at her new digs.

"It's awesome," she said in a whisper as soft and thankful as a prayer.

She had made it to college. It was the destination of a dream, but only the beginning of her new life. Plenty more challenges were looming.

Besides learning to adjust to college life, Mercedes felt the burden of worrying about her family.

"Are you doing okay?" she would message her younger brother, Marcus, who was starting his sophomore year of high school. "Do you have enough clothes?"

He assured her that he was fine. Her mother and grandmother, meanwhile, refused to take her calls or respond to her texts. Without the rent money from Mercedes, her grandmother had lost her apartment and moved in with the aunt. That left Mercedes feeling even more guilty.

Overwhelmed, Mercedes had a panic attack. She sought out her resident assistant and explained her dilemma.

"I don't know if I can do this," she said. "I miss my family."

Besides her guilt, she felt lonely. Because Mercedes didn't drink and didn't like to be around alcohol or drugs, she stayed away from the party scene. Maybe she was in the wrong place, after all.

She decided she would just give up, quit school, move back to Millville, and tend to her broken family. At eighteen, she would return to her long-standing role as parent and provider. College didn't seem like it was meant for a person like her.

She was packing her clothes in her dorm room when she took a call from Riccardo Dale, the Give Back scholar who made it his business to check in on the younger students and lend an emotional boost.

He had gotten word from Will that Mercedes was troubled. When Riccardo called Mercedes on FaceTime, he could see that she was emptying her closet and drawers.

"Why are you packing your things?" he asked.

"I'm going home," she told him.

Within moments, Riccardo was standing in her dorm room. He pleaded with her to give this some time.

She kept packing. But every time she would pack an item, Riccardo would pull it out.

He insisted that she hear him out. Riccardo talked about his own chaotic home life with an absent father and an addicted mother, breaking away, and then living with the guilt of going to college while loved ones were mired in trouble and going nowhere.

"There's nothing you can do to change things for them," he told her. "The best thing you can do is to take care of yourself."

Finally, Mercedes agreed to give it a chance. She saw a counselor regularly. And her deepening friendship with Will helped her find her moorings.

Mercedes and Will leaned on each other. They joked that they made the perfect team. The charismatic Will helped Mercedes with her social skills, while the studious Mercedes assisted Will with his academic chops.

The two of them would go on dates to a group Bible study on Fridays, with coffee afterward, and then go to church together on Sundays.

Before long, Mercedes was making a lot of friends. On weekends, Melissa would drive to Rowan and pick up Mercedes and take her back to her house. It was good to get some home-cooked meals. And the hugs didn't hurt, either.

Months passed before Mercedes would be able to communicate with her grandmother. In some ways, it was perhaps not surprising that the grandmother and other family members found it so difficult to let go of Mercedes. This was a family that knew profound tragedies.

"It seems that everyone around them dies or ends up in a ditch of some kind," said Melissa. "It's no wonder they don't want her to go away."

A few days before Thanksgiving, Mercedes sent Mom Maw a text to tell her she loved her and that she wanted to come and see her. Her grandmother responded with some excuses. It couldn't work.

But early on Thanksgiving Day, Mercedes, who was staying at Melissa's place, looked at her phone and was startled to see a text from her grandmother.

I woke up this morning, her grandmother had written to Mercedes, *and I felt thankful for you.*

Fighting back tears, Mercedes was immediately determined to go see her. Melissa happily agreed to drive her, and even baked an apple pie and gathered roses for Mercedes to take to her grandmother.

Mercedes walked in the door, with a soft "Hi." Her grandmother seemed shocked to see her. Mercedes walked over and wrapped her arms around her grandmother. And Mom Maw hugged back.

"I love you," Mercedes told her.

"I love you, too," Mom Maw replied. "How is college?"

Mercedes would get a chance to squeeze Marcus tight, tell him how proud he made her, and talk to him about applying to become a Give Back scholar and go to college.

She had missed her family so deeply. There were troubles, as ever, but these were her people. Mercedes had not expected to come back and find that everything had miraculously turned around – and that her mother was in a good and healthy place. But she had dared to hope it was true. And then her mom drifted into the room, talking in an exaggerated, overly dramatic manner, occasionally nodding off. She was high.

Mercedes gave her a hug and told her that she loved her.

When she was back on campus, Mercedes and her grandmother continued to text each day to say, *I love you.*

"Not a day goes by without us talking," said Mercedes.

She kept Mom Maw up to date about her school progress, and her grandmother told her she was very proud. Mercedes was taking a heavy course load: English, Math, Health Sciences, Sociology, and Western Civilization.

Among her scholarly accomplishments: She had composed and constructed a comparison between Buddhism and

Christianity and she had written a ten-page argumentative essay about the imperative to address climate change.

She even won a role in a play, *Blocks on a Shelf*, where she acted the role of a young woman who had known hardship.

Mercedes seemed to be finding her way. Life wasn't always easy. She would agonize about her schoolwork, worry about her family, have occasional panic attacks. But she was going to make it.

Melissa and Mercedes daydreamed about her future. Melissa thought it would be a good idea for Mercedes to study abroad for a semester, perhaps during her junior year. Maybe France? Or Italy? Possibly Australia?

Mercedes was wide-eyed about the exotic possibilities.

"I've been to Philly and that's about it," she said. "Wherever they'll take me, I'll go."

It was good to have her Give Back pals nearby on campus. Give Back even had an office on campus, with a 24-hour study room staffed by volunteers from the organization, including the former Give Back scholar-turned-staffer, Joshua Meekins.

Mercedes could always look to Riccardo, who was a couple of years older, for advice and example. And she had grown very fond of Will. The two of them had bonded during talks about the struggles in their childhoods and their dreams about the future. Who ever thought that they would find their way here?

"Sometimes I'll be walking with Will and I'll say, 'Dude, we're in college!' And he'll say, 'It's crazy. It's insane.'"

When the semester ended, Mercedes had earned straight As.

EPILOGUE

As the young people in this book demonstrate, there is no shortage of smarts and talent among those who have experienced foster care, homelessness, or the incarceration of a parent.

That such a small percentage of young people from these backgrounds attend college and earn a degree, however, is nothing less than a national shame.

But it is scarcely surprising. For foster children who are shuttled to home after home, school after school, trying to keep up with homework and tests, it can seem impossible. For those living with the poverty that often results from the incarceration of a parent, earning money for family survival becomes a more immediate concern than plotting a course to college, or even high school graduation.

The barriers these young people face cause many to conclude early in their lives that college is simply not meant for people like them. That message amounts to a breach in the social covenant that merit, not childhood circumstances, are what *should* really count.

Unfortunately, the importance of money as a predictor of going to college is staggering. Children in the upper 1 percent of income are seventy-seven times more likely to attend an Ivy League school than are students who are eligible for a Pell Grant. National news has revealed blatant cases of wealthy parents paying bribes to secure a spot for their children at a prestigious school. But those cases are a mere thimble in a sea of inequity. From the start, children from disadvantaged backgrounds are typically deprived of many of the educational and extracurricular bonuses that help an applicant gain entrance to college.

Indeed, about one in two community college students and one in three university students don't always have enough to eat and a similar percentage lack reliable housing, according to researchers at Wisconsin HOPE Lab and Temple University. These students often couch surf at the homes of friends or older adults, frequently putting themselves in risky circumstances.

While the roadblocks to college pose an unfairness for children of adversity, they also create problems for the larger society. Those without education are far more likely to be involved in the criminal justice system and require social services borne by the taxpayers.

And for those growing up in such adversity, now and tomorrow, where will they turn for mentors who can share their experiences? We need school teachers who grew up in hardship and can take aside a child and talk from personal knowledge about the challenges, struggles, and the possibilities of college.

Those possibilities *can* be realized. I have seen it firsthand. Of the 210 students selected for Give Back scholarships in the high school graduation class of 2019, some 97 percent were accepted to college. In the class of 2018, fully 100 percent of the 43 Give Back students entered college and remain in good standing.

While Give Something Back is devoted to do what we can to assist these young people, we recognize that we reach only a tiny fraction of those who need guidance and financial support in reaching higher education, whether that means a four-year university, community college, or a trade school—all of them respected paths that can lead to rewarding careers.

Government can do much more to ensure that students from hardship receive the mentoring and social support they need to stay on track, as well as the financial resources to pay for college. The business community, too, can step up to contribute to the cause.

They just might find a superstar who rose from adversity to join their ranks.

INDEX

Also by Robert Owen Carr with Dirk Johnson

*Through the Fires: An American Story of
Turbulence, Business Triumph and Giving Back*

*Working Class to College: The Promise and Peril
Facing Blue-Collar America*